Enterprise Mobility Management

Everything you need to know about MDM, MAM, and BYOD

Jack Madden

Enterprise Mobility Management

Everything you need to know about MDM, MAM, and BYOD

2013 Edition

Copyright © 2013 by Jack Madden

Published by
Jack Madden
San Francisco, California
www.brianmadden.com/emmbook

Written by
Jack Madden

Editor
Brian Madden

Copy Editor
Monica Sambataro

ISBN 978-9896506-0-1

First Printing, July 2013

Printed in the United States of America

Contents at a glance

Table of Contents

Foreword

In many ways my brother, Jack Madden, was destined to write this book. Having worked with Gabe Knuth and me on and off since 2005, Jack began as the "utility player" for BrianMadden.com and our BriForum conference.

But over time, our roles evolved. As Gabe and I continued to focus on desktop virtualization, we kept noticing that more and more of those dang "kids" wanted to do actual work on their new-fangled phones with no buttons. "Those are music-playing toys, not enterprise-grade tools!" Gabe and I would sigh while upgrading our corporate system to the latest version of BlackBerry Enterprise Server. "No iPhones in our office!"

Of course our naive feelings did not stem the tide of users wanting to use iOS and Android devices for work, and eventually even "old" people like us realized there was actually some utility to these things. In fact, these mobile devices even started creeping into our world, first as pocket-sized clients for VDI and remote desktops, and then as fully fledged business tools, as even Gabe and I realized that our iPhones and Android devices were actually cooler and more useful than the BlackBerrys we had been foisting on our users for the better part of a decade.

As luck would have it, that's right around the time that Jack joined our company full time. We initially envisioned that he'd be the "third guy" on our desktop virtualization team, meaning we naturally dumped whatever it was that we didn't want to deal with onto Jack.

Understanding mobile phones in the enterprise, tablets, iOS, and Android was the first thing we unloaded on him. We thought we dodged a bullet, but Jack relished it, realizing that he essentially won the lottery of the "right technology at the right time" game. I mean, here it was, mid-2011, and we made it Jack's full-time job to study, understand, figure out, debunk, and explain how enterprises deal with mobile devices. His only job was to learn and write about MDM, MAM, EMM, and BYOD.

And relish it he did! As I write this foreword in mid-2013, Jack has published over 150 articles on enterprise mobility on Brian-

Madden.com. He's talked to hundreds of IT pros, vendor executives, consultants, and end users in this space, and he's spoken about this topic at major events all over the world (including Citrix Synergy, VMworld, and BriForum).

So it's no surprise that last year, Jack came to us and said, "You know, there aren't any books on enterprise mobility management, and a lot of the articles about it on the web miss the point." Hello, opportunity! That single conversation over beers almost a year ago led to the book you're holding in your hands now.

Having read and edited multiple revisions, I can tell you that there is no single better resource on the planet for educating yourself on the intricacies and nuances of enterprise mobility management than this book, and there is no one better than Jack to have written it. He has contributed many original ideas to the EMM field over the past two years, and he's woven what you need to know into a single book that's educational while being very readable. Jack has also done a great job of focusing on the fundamentals of how EMM and mobile devices work, meaning you can apply what you learn here to your own environment regardless of which vendor's products you choose or how you design your implementation.

So whether you're in the early planning stages, the vendor selection phase, or your boss has simply told you to "go figure out BYOD," this book gets my highest recommendation for a place to start.

Brian Madden
July 2013

Preface

I spent the year and a half leading up to this book living and breathing the enterprise mobility management space, and I couldn't be any more excited about it!

How did I get to this point? In 2011, I joined Brian Madden and Gabe Knuth at TechTarget as "Blogger No. 3" for BrianMadden.com, after having worked behind the scenes with them on and off for several years. At the time, Brian and Gabe had just begun speaking and writing about the emerging trend of the consumerization of IT, and one of the first big projects after I came on was launching a new blog to cover the topic. By the beginning of 2012, I was given full reign over the new site, ConsumerizeIT.com.

Covering "consumerization" meant writing about a wide range of technologies and ideas, not the least of which were mobile device management (MDM), mobile app management (MAM), bring your own device (BYOD), and a ton of other technologies that collectively make up the area of enterprise mobility management (EMM), including app wrapping, mobile virtualization, email, and file syncing. In short order, I soon became our group's go-to person for anything related to EMM.

As 2012 went by, Brian, Gabe and I realized two things: First, we realized just how closely EMM is related to our traditional desktop virtualization coverage, so we recombined ConsumerizeIT.com and BrianMadden.com. Now we just consider it all "end-user computing." Second, we realized that there were a lot of people out there with questions about how all of these new EMM technologies actually work, and not many places to find the answers. The result of that realization is this book.

I want to thank Brian and Gabe and the rest of our group at TechTarget for helping make this book possible, the many people in the EMM industry who I've had a chance to meet and who have taught me so much, and the gang of BriForum presenters, who have always been an inspiration. I'd also especially like to thank the reviewers that gave me helpful comments and suggestions. Thanks, everybody! EMM rocks!

Jack Madden
@jackmadden
July 2013

Notes

iOS 7

Shortly before this book was published in June 2013, Apple announced some of the features of the newest version of the operating system that runs its mobile devices, iOS 7. Without a doubt, iOS 7 will bring significant changes for the enterprise. However, the beta version of iOS 7 and all of the details about its new enterprise features are available only to registered iOS developers and is subject to a nondisclosure agreement (NDA). The public release of iOS 7 is expected in the fall 2013.

There are a few new features and changes that Apple has discussed publicly, so those will be covered in this book where relevant. I'm going to avoid too much wild speculation about changes for which we have fewer details. The simple reality is that if you want to know more, you either have to wait until the public release in the fall or sign up for the iOS Developer Program.

Once iOS 7 is released and the NDA is lifted, I will be publishing an update to this book. If you've purchased the Amazon Kindle edition, the update will be available free of charge. In the meantime, you can keep up with the latest iOS 7 news by reading my blog at BrianMadden.com or following me on Twitter: @JackMadden.

Keep in mind that even with the potential changes, it will still be the same iOS as before and everything you read here will still apply. So you don't have to wait until iOS 7 is released to read this book—it will be just a few pages' worth of new material.

Vendor information

This book does not attempt to list or compare all of the EMM vendors that are active today. A few will be mentioned for specific reasons, but it would be impractical to attempt to cover them all here. Rest assured that the concepts in this book pertain to many different vendors. For more specific information about different EMM vendors, I'm happy to recommend the PQR EMM Smackdown white paper, by Peter Sterk and Ruben Spruijt (at www.pqr.com/whitepapers).

1. The Mobile World

Introduction

In August 2012 I attended a small one-day conference in New York exploring the way corporate IT was changing. I wasn't speaking that day, rather, I was just observing and talking to attendees and exhibitors and sort of keeping a low profile. I spoke with an attendee who learned I wrote about how IT departments deal with iPhones, Android phones, and tablets, and our conversation went something like this:

> Conference attendee: *So, Jack, you know about mobile? They said our company needs to secure our devices. What should we do? We need MDM* [mobile device management]. *Which one should I pick?*
>
> Me: *Oh, hi, nice to meet you. So what is it that you're—*
>
> Conference attendee: *We need MDM for our devices, don't we?*

Me: *Okay, what do you want to do with it? What do the employees at your company want to do with their devices? Email? Other things? Just get on the network, or access files?*

Conference attendee: *I don't know. We need to secure our phones with MDM. Which MDM should I pick?*

The conference attendee was clearly caught up in the idea that she needed to do *something* about managing the mobile devices in her organization, but she didn't have a good idea of how MDM technology works, what it does, and why exactly her company should deploy it (other than the overarching generic desire to "make our phones secure"). All she had heard was the hot buzz term: MDM. This was just one conversation, but it's the tip of the iceberg when it comes to confusion about managing mobility in the enterprise.

But can we blame anyone for being so confused? It happened so fast, after all. For years enterprise mobility meant "BlackBerrys." They were mostly used for email, and they were typically provided by employers. Corporate IT departments gave out all the phones, delivered email messages to them, and made sure they had proper security policies in place using BlackBerry Enterprise Server. It was simple. But then, in 2007, the iPhone (and later Android and the iPad) came along, and people wanted to use those devices for work instead. The problem was that when they first came out, they couldn't be controlled in the way the old BlackBerrys could.

By 2010, we finally had the technology to manage these new phones: mobile device management. But even so, there was still another big problem: Employees used these new devices in ways that were very different from how they used their old BlackBerrys, and many of these new phones were the employees' personal devices and not corporate-owned. (We use the term BYOD, or bring your own device, to describe the practice of employees bringing their own phones and tablets into the office to use for work.)

The confusion doesn't end at MDM and BYOD, however. In the past year or two, there has been yet another wave of new technology to address the new devices: mobile app management

(MAM), software that enables corporate IT departments to manage only a few individual mobile apps, rather than entire devices.

But wait, there's more! In addition to MDM, BYOD and MAM, now we also have mobile information management (MIM), profiles, file syncing, mobile email management (MEM), data loss protection, mobile virtualization, app wrapping, app signing, certificates, app stores, Exchange ActiveSync, and something called COPE (corporate owned, personally enabled). All of these things are collectively referred to as enterprise mobility management (EMM). More importantly, you can see that the stage is set for a confused market!

Fortunately for you, you're holding this book in your hands right now! You'll learn what all of these things are, how they work, and why they may (or may not) be important to you. By the end of the book, you'll be equipped to ask—and hopefully answer—all the important questions about EMM.

Why are we here?

While this book aims to clear up confusion around EMM technologies, there's a more important question: Why are we here talking about enterprise mobility in the first place? The answer involves much more than MDM or MAM or BYOD, and requires us to look beyond these specific technologies.

Part of why we're here is this concept known as "the consumerization of IT." I'll explain more about this in a little bit, but the basic idea is that these days, users can access incredible tools, devices, and services that are, in many ways, more advanced than the tools that IT provides to them. Once users get a taste of these awesome tools in their personal lives, they inevitably want to start using them for work, too. If we (as IT) don't recognize that, we're set to be in for a rough time!

But really the consumerization of IT is just a symptom of the true reason why we're here: the completely revolutionary wave of mobility advancement that came with the iPhone, Android, iPads, 3G and 4G, mobile apps, software as a service (SaaS), and dozens of other related technologies.

I'm not going to go on too long about how awesome all this stuff is, because we're all living it every day. It'll just suffice to say that the real reason I wrote this book (and why you're reading it) is that our smartphones and tablets do lots of cool things that make our work and personal lives more connected and productive.

I'm making a point of this right now so that later on, when I get deep into the minutiae of corporate mobility and dealing with users, you can remember that we're in a pretty great place. The technical particulars are simply ways to enable more people to take advantage of this.

The Seven Universal Truths of Enterprise Mobility in 2013

People have been talking about enterprise mobility for years, and there are many opinions about the state of the industry and mobility in general. In order to put together this book, I had to make some assumptions so that we can all start from the same place. So for the purposes of this book and mobility in 2013, I believe the following seven truths apply to enterprise mobility. These are not up for discussion, but are rather the foundational concepts for the rest of this book.

Truth 1: We can put the "Are tablets toys or work devices?" debate to bed.

When iPhones and Android phones first came out, and especially when the iPad first arrived, there was a lot of debate about whether these consumer devices had a place in the enterprise, or if they were merely "toys." Of course, regardless of what some analysts said, people brought them into work anyway, and the debate ended pretty quickly. Today, anyone who says an iPad is just a toy will get laughed out of the room. Sure, there are places where devices with keyboards and mice and huge displays are still far superior for getting work done, and I'm not saying iPads will replace laptops.

But we can now all be confident that there's a place for tablets and for phones that do more than just make calls and send emails. Nowadays, whichever device a particular user favors is a matter of personal preference. Some people might see iPad users fumbling around with these little origami-like stands and Bluetooth keyboards and think they look silly, while other people are overjoyed at the thought of never having to carry a big heavy laptop around. Either opinion is fine, though, and really it's none of our business. The fact is that mobile devices of all shapes and sizes are used as legitimate business tools, and IT needs to find ways to work with them.

Truth 2: Thanks to the consumerization of IT, users now can do whatever they want.

As consumer-oriented technology has been making huge leaps and bounds, users have become accustomed to working with incredibly powerful, fast, and rapidly changing software and devices. But then when those users come into work, what are they faced with? Older, slower enterprise IT technology that changes at a seemingly glacial pace. Armed with all their great personal technology, though, employees can now just ignore the resources IT gives them and use their own tools.

There are so many examples of this: Users faced with a slow Wi-Fi connection or a restrictive corporate network that disallows certain sites can tether to their 4G LTE mobile phone instead. Users fed up with waiting for mapped network drives to load can save their files to Dropbox. Users dealing with a full mailbox quota and small attachment size limit can forward their work emails to Gmail. Every single consumer-oriented app, website, and service provides an opportunity for users to forget what IT gives them and work in their own way. Often, IT has no idea that this is going on, and even when it does, in many cases there's nothing it can do about it!

This is the *real* story of the consumerization of IT. There was a lot of resistance and pushback to this concept when it was first introduced, but now it's 2013, and most everybody acknowledges that these situations are happening. There's even a special term to describe this new environment: *fuit*, the Latin word meaning "he, she or it was." As in, "IT was in control of users, but it no longer is." But also spell it out: F.U.I.T. Get it?

Truth 3: Consumerization isn't going away, but at least the difficult part has passed.

The good news in most cases is that users aren't actively trying to say "FU" to IT—they're just trying to do their jobs, and they usually don't even know that what they're doing may not be secure or isn't the official corporate way. Unfortunately, when it comes to consumerization, the smoke is out of the bottle and there's no way of putting it back in. Ignoring the consumerization of IT doesn't make it go away, and no amount of wishing, crying, or begging will change it.

That said, I strongly believe the hard part has passed us by. Remember that before all of this consumerization stuff happened (think decades ago), the technology users had at work was far more advanced than what they had at home. But in today's world, users go out and buy technology for home that's way more advanced than what they get at work, so at some point we had this inversion. Luckily this inversion was a one-time event. While it was happening, it wasn't always easy to recognize, and things got chaotic for a while and FUIT happened. We can be forgiven for not recognizing it immediately, because after all, when had something like this happened to us in IT before?

Now we can breathe a sigh of relief—we know where we stand. There may be some huge jumps in technology that take us by surprise, but it won't be as much of a problem because the inversion of consumer and corporate technology is now safely in the past. It would be an impossible task to keep up with the rapid pace of consumer technology—not to mention that it would also require an enormous IT budget! But now we know what can happen when the gap between corporate IT and consumer technology grows too wide. Dealing with the consumerization of IT today means making a good-faith effort to mind the gap between the two in order to (hopefully) prevent FUIT from happening again.

Truth 4: It doesn't take BYOD to get modern smartphones.

In the early days, just about all iPhone and Android phones were personal devices, while the standard corporate-issued phones were BlackBerrys. (Remember, some people even thought these new devices were just toys!)

But today, an iPhone or Android phone is just as likely to be purchased and paid for by a company as by an end user. We can no longer make the assumption that an iPhone or Android phone or even an iPad is a personal device.

Truth 5: There is a difference between CoIT and BYOD.

Since many of the issues around the consumerization of IT (CoIT) emerged at the same time as—and partly because of—BYOD, a lot of people use the two terms interchangeably. But the reality is that device ownership (corporate versus employee) and how "consumerization friendly" management policies are (completely locked down versus wide open) are independent variables. With these two variables, there are four possible combinations:

- Yes BYOD, Yes CoIT (Wide-open personal devices)
- No BYOD, Yes CoIT (Wide-open corporate devices)
- No BYOD, No CoIT (Locked-down corporate devices)
- Yes BYOD, No CoIT (Locked-down personal devices)

Yes BYOD, Yes CoIT

This is probably what most people have in mind when they consider BYOD. The users pay for their own devices and phone bills, which can be any device they want. IT might provide some access to corporate resources, but generally users are free to do whatever they want with their devices.

No BYOD, Yes CoIT

Here the company pays for the devices, but otherwise users still get a lot of freedom over how they use them. This is also known by the term COPE (corporate owned, personally enabled). If your company supports it, this is probably one of the nicest ways to work.

No BYOD, No CoIT

This is how corporate phones have been since the BlackBerry days. The company provides the devices, but also locks them down as it sees fit. The difference now is, thanks to MDM technology, instead of just BlackBerrys, corporate devices can be iPhones or Android devices, too. Sure, these devices are cool because of their touchscreens and high performance and everything, but if they're locked down, users will be missing out on a lot of the reasons why these are so popular in the first place.

Yes BYOD, No CoIT

This is the worst. Somebody has the idea of, "Hey, our company understands that our young, hip workers want to use their gadgets, so from now on, no more BlackBerrys. Everyone can bring in their own phone instead!" But then if the company also decides that everybody's phone needs to be totally locked down to access corporate resources, now the users have to get a second phone to actually have fun on. This is really just shifting the phone bills over to the users.

Truth 6: You'll always have to deal with some amount of BYOD.

Personal devices are an issue that any company will have to deal with, no matter what. You can buy your users all the tablets and whatever smartphones they want, but in these days of rapid device churn, there will always be personal devices that access corporate resources. You just can't move as fast as geeky users who visit the electronics store. BYOD will happen no matter what.

Truth 7: BYOD doesn't matter as much anymore.

As you read this book, you'll notice that after the introduction, I'm going to mostly be silent on the issue of BYOD until the end of the book. That's because employees expect an iPhone to be an iPhone no matter who buys it. (Blame consumerization!) This in turn means you have to support users' desires on their iPhones regardless of whether they're corporate issued or brought in by employees. In other words, who cares whether that iPhone is BYOD or yours—you still have to deal with it in basically the same way, which means about 95% of what we cover in this book applies to all devices regardless of who owns them.

What Else Will This Book Cover?

This book is for anyone who's noticed the buzz around enterprise mobility management. It's for people who've heard of MDM and want to know how it works. It's for people who have observed the debate between MDM and MAM vendors and want to know how they fit together. It's for people who've heard ominous warnings about the dangers of BYOD and want to see what the big deal is.

This book also is for users who want to understand what their company is doing to their device with MDM. And it's for developers who want to fit their apps into EMM structures.

And finally, this book is for companies that for years have dealt with only BlackBerry and BlackBerry Enterprise Server (BES) and want to figure out what's next. It's for desktop people who are now tasked with delivering applications and data to new platforms. It's for the mobile managers who were happy with BES for the past 10 years and now have to deal with users bringing in iPhones.

What this book is not about

There are some important areas around enterprise mobility that *won't* be covered in this book.

I won't be talking much about app strategy—with the exception of some core apps like file syncing clients, email clients, browsers, and a few others. I won't be addressing which other apps to mobilize or what features to include in your mobile apps or anything like that. (Though I will cover how to deploy, manage, and integrate these apps into your EMM system once you decide on them.) I won't be talking about anything related to app development except for the products that allow developers to include management hooks in their apps.

This book also won't be about hard-core security with a capital S, so no "by exploiting this bug here with this app, then there's a buffer overflow over there and then you can use this weakness here to run unsigned code on this device, and by impersonating this call..." and so on. That's certainly a very important subject, but it's beyond our present scope.

Finally, I won't be talking about mobile devices versus keyboards and mice, what platforms are good for content consumption versus content creation, or the best way for users to work. I'll just assume that, thanks to the effects of consumerization, you want to have a proactive attitude toward supporting all the ways your users want to work.

What this book will talk about instead

In this book, I'm going to concentrate on the EMM products that have emerged in the past few years. This means MDM, MAM, MIM, email, BYOD, and other related technologies. I'm assuming that everyone has to deal with email, file syncing, web apps that you want in a secure browser, and mobile apps (both internally and externally created). Combine that with users who don't want accessing corporate resources on their phone to affect their experience and you have all the pieces that I'll be taking into account over the rest of the book.

2. How Our Present Mobile Landscape Came to Be

Looking around right now, we realize that the mobile device landscape is pretty exciting. We all got used to iPhones and Android phones and tablets really fast. Sure, every year brings small improvements, but the iPhone, iPad, and Android can be collectively seen as an example of a once-per-decade revolution.

But now that the iPhone is 6 years old, Android is 5, and the iPad is 3, users have settled in. There's even been a little disappointment as people are realizing that advancements in phones and tablets are now in a slower, more incremental stage. Remember how disappointed everyone was when the iPhone 5 was "merely" faster and lighter and had a bigger screen? Microsoft might be hoping that Windows 8 convertible devices are the basis for the next revolution, but good luck to them—we'll check back in a year or two to see if that actually happens.

Even though this round of big changes has already happened on the device side, the enterprise mobility management world is still catching up. Initially, there was the gap in the actual management technology itself. It wasn't until 2010 that any of the new devices approached the manageability of BlackBerry, and truth be told, there's still a big gap (but I'll get into that later). Second, even after mobile device management technology emerged, we still faced the reality of consumerization, leaving a gap between the old management styles the original MDM products were built around and the new way that users work.

This chapter will cover the manageable BlackBerry world that existed before iPhones, the chaos associated with the iPhone's rise, and the journey toward the MDM technology that arose in 2010.

Enterprise Mobility Before the iPhone

iPhones and Android are synonymous with the idea of the smartphone, but really, we already had smartphones before them: Black-Berrys. (And we shouldn't forget that there was also a bunch of other devices running Windows Mobile, PalmOS, and Symbian.) It's easy to forget that those pre-iPhoneian devices had third-party apps, browsers, cameras, and music players—all things that are now strongly associated with iPhones and Android phones.

Even more important than the introduction of those features was the earlier revolution that came with having mobile email in the first place. So even though the introduction of iPhones and Android heralded a new epoch, the devices they replaced had signaled their own epoch several years earlier. Of all of those devices, BlackBerry was the dominant platform, so let's take a quick look back at it.

The Blackberry world

Unlike the smartphones we have today, BlackBerry started out solidly as a platform for the enterprise. These phones always catered to professionals, with the appropriate management and security features built in from the beginning. Research In Motion (RIM) created the first BlackBerry mobile email device, the pager-like 850, in 1999. The device automatically kept completely in sync with users' desktops and alerted users of new messages on the device via push notifications. The Black-Berry email device was combined with a phone for the first time in 2002, and the secure enterprise-manageable smartphone was born.

It's probably redundant to say it now, but these things were a huge deal. Throughout the middle of the decade, we saw trends like the emergence of the term *CrackBerry*. These devices were blamed for ruining people's work and life balance, pundits wondered about the impact of constant connectivity, people talked about getting injuries from thumb typing, and there were some people who had pretty bad manners with them. You know the rest of the story. It's basically the same as with any other new communications technology.

BlackBerrys spread throughout the corporate world and even into high-security areas like government, changing the way all sorts of professionals did their jobs, in many of the same ways the iPhone would change the lives of consumers (and professionals) a few years later. But Blackberrys of the early 2000s were pretty much for people's work lives. Most BlackBerry users had separate mobile phones for personal use.

Of course personal phones were very different then, too. For example, think back to the old Motorola Razr flip phone, one of the most popular phones of all time. Sure, there were some consumer phones in the mid-2000s that had email and primitive browsers or could play music, but the most important features for consumers back then were small size and maybe a camera (though no one would have considered using it to replace an ordinary camera). People were getting their music from iPods, their photos from a digital camera, and any data from text messages. BlackBer-ry didn't push hard into this consumer world until the late-2000s.

Keep in mind that even after the introduction the iPhone and Android, BlackBerrys were quite popular, too.

Under the covers of the Blackberry world

BlackBerrys and their management and messaging platform, BlackBerry Enterprise Server (BES), were enterprise devices and enterprise software from the beginning. As enterprise software, Blackberry's primary concern was manageability, security, and reliability, not the flashy, fad-driven consumer world. These devices were issued to users by IT departments that set everything up and provided training, just like with other business tools, such as laptops, copy machines, and coffee makers.

Using BES, almost every single aspect of a BlackBerry's functionality could be managed by IT over the air (no need to physically connect to a desktop). Many of the fundamental concerns back then were the same ones that MDM vendors talk about today: making sure the device is encrypted, being able to wipe all the data off of a device remotely if it is lost or stolen, requiring a user to enter a password, and being able to provision email account, VPN, and Wi-Fi settings.

In addition to the BlackBerry's corporate legacy, remember that much of its rise happened very close to the time of the corporate accountability scandals of the early 2000s. Resulting regulations, such as Sarbanes-Oxley, were a lot closer at that time than now (not to say that it's not a concern today, but that it was just fresher then). And BlackBerry management features reflected the era.

Also remember that the Blackberry was "vertically integrated," since RIM built the device hardware, the device's OS, the management server, and the software that carriers used to connect the Blackberrys to the airwaves. Because of all this, there was no gap between the introduction of a new device feature and the introduction of the ability to manage it. As you'll see, this is very much in contrast to today, where EMM vendors scramble to add functionality onto consumer-oriented platforms that are updated frequently.

BES was like a lot of other enterprise software—multiple servers, components, services, and consoles to install—something very different from the push-button instant setup of many SaaS-based EMM solutions today. It was complicated (but powerful), and with BES and Blackberrys, IT *knew* it was in control and precisely what it could control. And users? Well, they just used it. When something broke, they went to the helpdesk, just like they would with a laptop.

This is what MDM was like for almost a decade—just like managing any other enterprise system. And this is the exact functionality that many people sought to replicate when iOS and Android came out.

BlackBerry competitors

Even though we hold up BlackBerry as being *the* pre-iPhone device and MDM and mobile email platform, there were still several competitors back then. Microsoft Windows Phone and Windows Mobile, PalmOS and webOS, and Symbian were all major players in the smartphone world as well.

Microsoft

While the Windows Phone mobile OS is a small niche today, Windows Mobile (as it used to be called) is significant for two reasons. First, Windows Mobile devices were for a time major competition to the BlackBerry. Second, Exchange ActiveSync (EAS)—the management and email protocol developed by Microsoft for Windows Mobile—is now the de facto standard for modern mobile devices and mail clients.

Today's Windows Phone devices can trace their lineage back to the first Windows CE handheld devices in 1996. Windows CE became the Pocket PC 2000, and the first phones running Pocket PC came in 2002. The Windows Mobile name came in 2003, and continued to be used as the platform evolved through 2009. As the devices and OS progressed, so did EAS, which was introduced in 2002 as way to sync Exchange email to smartphones. Aside from delivering messages and syncing mailboxes, Exchange ActiveSync provided over-the-air management of mobile device security settings.

The height of Windows Mobile popularity happened in 2006 and 2007, with a 42% share of smartphone sales in 2007. The height of manageability was reached slightly later with Windows Mobile 6.1 and 6.5 devices combined with the version of EAS that came with Exchange 2007 SP1 and System Center Mobile Device Manager 2008. Microsoft over-the-air control went so far as covering third-party applications, something that's even kind of difficult with modern MDM. Administrators could also control things like encryption and passwords, the devices could be wiped remotely in case they were lost, and general management capabilities were pretty good. (Though they weren't ever at the same level as the BlackBerry.)

In 2010, Microsoft went in a different direction with Windows Phone 7. It was aimed at the consumer market, but unfortunately for Microsoft, the consumer market was already being dominated by the iPhone and Android. Windows Mobile 7 didn't offer any backward compatibility with earlier versions of Windows Mobile, and almost all of the management features were dropped. In general, it was a pretty dark time for Microsoft mobile operating systems.

Windows Phone 8 in 2012 was a complete departure from the Windows Phone 7 and Windows Mobile platform. It was based on the Windows NT kernel, giving it better compatibility with Windows 8. Microsoft also added many security features back in, which means that Windows Phone 8 management capabilities are now on par with iOS and Android.

PalmOS/webOS

PalmOS (which later evolved to "webOS") is another notable casualty of the disruption caused by the iPhone. Palm's operating system, PalmOS, had been around since the mid-1990s in a range of PDAs and later phones. Some of the Palm smartphones, like the Treo, were fairly popular alternatives to BlackBerry and Windows Mobile devices in the mid-2000s. In 2009, Palm replaced it with webOS, and introduced the Palm Pre and Palm Pixi as iPhone and Android competitors. In 2010, Palm was acquired by Hewlett-Packard, and they released the Pre 2 smartphone. By most accounts the Pre 2 wasn't terrible, but the webOS-based tablet that HP released in 2011 was.

WebOS devices supported very few EAS policies, including remote wipe, remote locking, and password policies. WebOS 2 with the Pre 2 added VPN support, and a 2.1 update added encryption, but that was it.

Symbian

Throughout the 2000s, Symbian phones made by Nokia and others were a part of the smartphone landscape as well, generally much more significant globally than in the U.S. Nokia struck a deal with Microsoft in 2011 to make all of its phones run Windows Phone, and with that Symbian had no more visibility in the U.S. Symbian was also extremely popular for non-smartphones as well, but now for that use case it's gradually being replaced by Android.

Symbian can be managed through EAS and third-party agent applications, and many of the older MDM providers still support it. Policies include encryption, passwords, remote lock, and remote wipe; and Symbian also supports mobile VPNs.

Enter the iPhone and Android

While BlackBerry was dominating the business world in the mid-2000s, Apple was having enormous success with MP3 players. After a long decline from the late 1980s to the late 90s, Apple was ascending again with a string of landmarks that consumers loved: the iMac in 1998; OS X, the first Apple stores, and the iPod in 2001; the iTunes store in 2003; and Intel-based Macs in 2006.

It was in this world—where everyone had a corporate Black-Berry for work email and an iPod for music, and where "mobile computing" meant "email on phones and everything else on a laptop"—that the iPhone was born on June 29, 2007. What was so special about the iPhone? After all, at the time lots of other phones already had browsers, cameras, and MP3 players. (Other phones also had plenty of features that the iPhone didn't have: third-party apps, 3G connectivity, and support for corporate email and management.) What the iPhone did have was Apple's way of making many of these features actually usable for the first time, plus several years of iPod, iTunes, and Mac popularity to build on.

The iPhone eventually gained the initial features it was missing (and many more), but what really matters is the familiar story about how the iPhone changed the face of mobile computing. It was a revolution that nobody could have predicted. When people first began hearing rumors about a phone from Apple, everybody thought it would look like existing phones, or some odd mash-up of flip phone and iPod. (And, in fact, there were a few phones with iTunes clients in 2005—but you know how those worked out!) When Steve Jobs announced the iPhone on January 9, 2007, he told the audience at the event that Apple was releasing three new products: a "widescreen iPod with touch controls, a revolutionary mobile phone, and a breakthrough Internet communications device." The big surprise came when he revealed that all three of these were one single device. (Look this up on YouTube.) Needless to say, this was a big moment.

The iPhone laid the groundwork so that we knew what to expect when the first Android phone, the HTC Dream, arrived in October 2008. There were some major differences, though. To begin with, most of the early Android devices had physical keyboards, and Android didn't have years of iPod popularity to use as a launching platform.

The most important difference for Android was that the entire distribution model was completely different from the way that the iPhone was distributed. Android was first started in 2003 and was purchased by Google in 2005. By 2007, it was part of a mobile industry consortium called the Open Handset Alliance. Android is open source and can be freely modified by each different phone maker, so the complete vertical integration that the iPhone takes advantage of just isn't there. This has its advantages and disadvantages, and as we look at mobile device management, they'll become clear. Overall, though, the feeling when Android came out was one of, "Okay, we've seen this before with Apple. Now let's see Google's take on it."

Around the same time, BlackBerry responded to the iPhone by releasing the BlackBerry Bold in November 2008. Many of the technical specifications were better than the iPhone, and it indeed enjoyed several years of success, but it still had a keyboard and suffered the fact that it just wasn't an iPhone. BlackBerry's attempts at devices with full-size touchscreens during that time were largely unsuccessful.

Overall, we associate the introduction of the iPhone with the death of the BlackBerry, but in reality, it took a couple of years for Android and iOS to completely dominate the smartphone market. Thanks to the general rise of smartphone sales, 2008 through 2010 were actually continued years of growth for Blackberry.

It was in 2011 that things really deteriorated for BlackBerry. The iPhone 4 had recently introduced over-the-air management capabilities that finally made it more acceptable for corporate environments, and BlackBerry was having trouble coming up with anything that could divert sales from iPhones and Android.

While all that was going on, Windows Mobile (and later Windows Phone) market share nearly disappeared and webOS disappeared completely. More recently, Android expanded down market to feature phones and largely replaced Symbian for smartphones in international markets. Some people thought that Android would be the iPhone killer, but it was really the killer of Windows Mobile and Symbian.

Problems with iPhones and Android

Today, we think of managing iPhones, Android, and personal devices as a significant issue that has to be dealt with. But back in their earliest days, they were just a blip on the radar for IT, like any other personal phone. Soon enough, though, two sets of problems emerged: the lack of management features and the challenges of consumerization.

When the iPhone and Android were initially released, there were absolutely no provisions for the types of corporate management policies that had been in place for years on BlackBerry and Windows Mobile. It would take a few years for Apple and Google to add these capabilities, and by the time they were eventually added, the way users interacted with their phones had changed so much that the old management models they emulated weren't adequate.

That change in the users was thanks to the consumerization of IT. Consumer technology was getting more powerful, social, and immersive, and it was only natural that users wanted to use their great personal tools for work, too. The iPhone and Android phones were the perfect embodiment of this trend. Without adequate management tools, when these devices came into the workplace, corporate data could leak out.

A Guided History of Management Features in iOS and Android

Today, we takev for granted that iOS and Android have mobile device management features, but it wasn't always like this, and it didn't happen overnight. Here I'm going to take a step back to look at how all of these features for corporate management evolved. Personally, I find this fascinating (really!), but if you don't care about which enterprise features came in which versions, then feel free to skip this section.

2007

The Apple iPhone was first announced in January 2007 and released that June. When it debuted, it was solidly a consumer device, more closely related to an MP3 player than to the enterprise. There was no way to manage it, and without support for Exchange ActiveSync (EAS) or BlackBerry Enterprise Server, it was completely ignored by IT. The iPhone did support POP and IMAP email, so technically it could be used with Exchange if a company chose to turn those on. (And hey, there was always Outlook Web Access, too!) But in general, since there was no way to enforce any management policies, only high-power executives got corporate email on their iPhones. So when Apple said the iPhone supported Exchange, it was a bit of a stretch.

There were other reasons why the original iPhone wasn't considered a "corporate" phone: It had to be activated and synced with iTunes, and how many IT departments would have allowed iTunes on users' computers at the time? The iPhone was also expensive and available only from a few carriers in each country.

Still, the browser—and the fact that it was actually usable—did make the iPhone valuable for some corporate users. And while there were no third-party apps yet, it did have a built-in VPN client. Even though most conventional knowledge in 2007 said the iPhone was not appropriate for corporate use, there already were people who were saying it was a great phone and a great work tool, and that companies would be well served by trying to figure out how to support it.

2008

Apple announced and released the beta of the second version of the iPhone's operating system (at the time it was just called iPhone OS 2) in March 2008, and announced the second-generation hardware (iPhone 3G) in June, releasing both in July. This was a huge deal, because iPhone OS 2 supported Microsoft EAS for corporate email and something called "configuration profiles" to manage phone settings. (And don't forget, iPhone OS 2 could also support third-party apps, developed using the newly released iPhone SDK.)

For corporate users, EAS support meant that email, calendars, contacts, and global address lookup could be accessed from the iPhone, though there wasn't yet support for other features like tasks, the ability to create meetings, out-of-office notifications, or follow-up flags.

More important, EAS brought a degree of over-the-air management to iPhones for the first time. IT could now remotely wipe and enforce password policy, though there wasn't yet support for device encryption. Even though that was still a problem for many environments, there were sweeping declarations of "Hurray! Now the iPhone is a corporate phone!" (Of course, the next time more advancements came around, there were even more sweeping declarations of its corporate acceptability: "Okay, guys, this time we *really* mean it's a corporate phone!") Naturally, thanks to the consumerization of IT, employee demand brought these devices into the workplace anyway, regardless of whether or not analysts considered them to be "corporate-ready."

The configuration profiles introduced in iPhone OS 2 later become the basis for many future iOS MDM advancements. Configuration profiles are XML files that specify settings for a range of security and administrative features on the device. When it added configuration profile support to iPhones, Apple also introduced the iPhone Configuration Utility, a tool for creating profiles. Configuration profiles could be installed via email attachments, downloaded from a server, or installed onto a device directly using a USB cable.

Initially, configuration profiles didn't contain any provisions for over-the-air management, but that could be provided by EAS instead. So really, they were more a matter of convenience because they didn't do much that users couldn't already do in the user interface.

The first profiles contained settings for passcode policy, Wi-Fi, VPN, POP and IMAP mail accounts, Exchange accounts, and carrier access point name settings (these determine how the device connects to the telecom data network, something that's usually not a concern for most MDM situations). Profiles could also be used to install certificates on devices, and the profiles themselves could be signed. All of these settings and credentials installed by a profile got removed from the device if the profile was removed.

What wasn't in profiles was a way to change any of these settings over the air, force a profile to be installed, lock a profile to a device, or restrict third-party apps or any other aspect of a device's behavior.

The third-party app market that was introduced was tightly controlled by Apple (all apps had to be approved and signed), but the iPhone Developer Enterprise Program provided a way for companies to develop and sign in-house apps on their own, as well as the ability to distribute apps to users via provisioning profiles. (App signing will be covered in depth in Chapters 3 and 4.)

Overall, while there were huge enterprise improvements in iPhone OS 2, there were still stumbling blocks for enterprises. One issue was that the devices had to be activated with iTunes, and there was nothing stopping users from running major software updates on their devices on their own, making it harder for IT to test new versions like it used to. Users could also back up and restore devices on their own, another security risk. Finally, the lack of encryption meant that the iPhone was still a "no-go" for many regulated industries. (And the iPhone was still available only through a single carrier in most markets.)

Meanwhile, in the Android world, 2008 saw the release of the first Android SDK in September and the first device, the HTC Dream, in October. Android had management challenges right from the beginning due to its open distribution model, as Google left many of the security and management features up to the discretion of device makers.

Unlike the iPhone, Android launched with third-party apps, but in terms of enterprise support, Android was way behind the iPhone. Even in 2008, the core Android Open Source Project (which is what I'm looking at in this timeline) didn't have any support for Exchange email, EAS policies, or any other management.

2009

Apple released the iPhone OS 3 beta and SDK in March 2009, while the third generation of the hardware, the iPhone 3GS, was announced in early June 2009 and released later that month.

There were a few new important management features, including the ability to encrypt an iPhone, more restrictions around its behavior, and the ability to prevent configuration profiles from being removed. General new features included cut, copy, and paste, the MobileMe service (which allowed end users to locate and wipe lost iPhones), and the Apple Push Notification Service.

A new "device restrictions" feature in configuration profiles included policies for blocking explicit content, the Safari browser, the YouTube app, buying music in the iTunes store, downloading apps from the Apple App Store, and the camera. Other features included the ability to ensure that backups were encrypted, and the ability to add web clips (shortcuts), LDAP lookup, and calendar subscriptions.

Over-the-air management was still limited to Exchange ActiveSync, but now with encryption and restrictions, the iPhone could be locked down to a considerable degree. These features allowed even more enterprises to support the iPhone. Users, on the other hand, continued to run amok.

For Android, version 1.6 in September 2009 added VPN support (though at the time there were already third-party VPN apps), and Android 2.0 in October brought support for Exchange ActiveSync. Unfortunately, there was no way to enforce any EAS security policies, and Android remained way behind iOS when it came to management features.

From these early years of Android—and to a lesser but still significant degree, iOS as well—third-party email clients gave a way to provide security features not offered by the OS. (Third-party clients had been around since before iOS and Android, and even today with smartphones supporting all the important EAS security policies, third-party email apps are still important as a way to keep corporate data isolated from personal applications.)

The first corporate email clients for Android actually appeared right when it was first launched in 2008. These included Nitrodesk Touchdown and Moxier Mail.

In the earlier days of the iPhone, Apple didn't allow any third-party apps that duplicated the functionality of built-in apps, so it wasn't until late 2009 that any third-party mail apps for iOS came along. Even once that happened, though, Apple didn't approve any apps that used Exchange ActiveSync, so early apps, like those from Good Technology (Good released its mail apps for both Android and iOS in December 2009), had to rely on other management protocols. It wasn't until 2011 that the first third-party EAS clients appeared in the Apple App Store.

2010

In 2010, there were major advancements for both Android and iOS, and it was a huge year for MDM. In fact, it wouldn't be a stretch to say that the Android and iOS changes in 2010 launched the modern mobile device management industry.

Apple announced the beta for iOS 4 (renamed from iPhone OS after the iPad was introduced) in April, and iPhone 4 was announced and released in June. iOS 4 included more options for device restrictions, but by far the most important new feature was the ability to manage devices and profiles wirelessly over the air.

Remember that before iOS 4, the only way to manage devices wirelessly over the air was through the fairly limited capabilities provided by EAS. iOS 4 brought a whole new range of over-the-air management capabilities: For one, it gave IT the ability to manage configuration profiles—and all of their associated settings—over the air. Second, it gave an alternative way to manage the device that was much richer than EAS.

Installing enterprise-signed apps became much easier with iOS 4, too. Instead of needing a USB cable and iTunes or the iPhone Configuration Utility, in-house apps could now be installed wirelessly by using manifest files.

Finally, there were a few new device restrictions, including the ability to prevent screen capture, automatic mail syncing while roaming, voice dialing while locked, and in-app purchases.

Over in the world of Android, in May 2010 Google announced Android 2.2, which introduced the Device Administration API. This API allows an application to enforce device-level management policies, including password requirements and device locking and wiping. This meant that it was possible to build MDM apps that did the basics of over-the-air management without having to rely on device manufactures to build the features on their own. Android 2.2 also brought the Android Cloud to Device Messaging Service (C2DM)—now known as Google Cloud Messaging—a gateway for sending push notifications to inactive apps. This gave MDM servers a way to interact with their agent applications and to enforce management actions remotely.

2011

While 2010 was the banner year for MDM, both platforms continued to make subsequent advancements.

The beta for iOS 5 introduced iCloud, Siri, over-the-air OS updates, and the ability to activate devices without using iTunes. July brought the Volume Purchasing Program for Business and the Custom B2B program, a way for developers to use the Apple App Store to distribute apps to select audiences. The iPhone 4S was announced and released in October 2011.

One of the biggest new MDM features in iOS 5 was the concept of "managed apps." MDM servers could now command devices to install and remove public or in-house apps. (However, users still have to accept the installation of MDM-managed apps, and MDM servers cannot remove user-installed apps.)

Android 3.0 gave the Device Administration API the ability to enforce more complex password policies and device encryption, and in October, Android 4.0 added camera control to the API.

2012

The biggest iOS management news of 2012 was the debut of the Apple Configurator, a utility from Apple that backs up iOS device images, creates golden images for mass deployments, and "supervises" devices. (Supervising devices with the Apple Configurator means checking users' images in and out on different devices, returning devices to a baseline state, installing apps, etc.)

This was followed up by the iOS 6 beta in June. In iOS 6, devices supervised using the Apple Configurator can be locked down to a single app, use a global HTTP proxy, and have a few more feature restrictions.

iOS 6 also revamped privacy settings, allowing users to have per-app control over access to photos, calendars, contacts, and reminders. The iPhone 5 itself was announced and released in September 2012.

2013

iOS 7 was introduced in June 2013, promising many new enterprise features. At the time of this writing, iOS 7 is in beta, and most of the details about it are covered by a nondisclosure agreement and currently available only to registered iOS developers.

The new features relevant to enterprises that Apple has discussed publicly include making multitasking available to all apps, push notifications for waking apps or prompting background tasks, the introduction of AirDrop (wireless device-to-device file transfers), automatic app updates, and Activation Lock (to discourage theft, the Apple ID associated with a device is now required to reactivate a device after it's wiped).

There are also features that Apple has given hints about but has not discussed publicly, including app-level VPNs, changes to app license management and the Volume Purchase Program, enterprise single sign-on, wireless app configuration, and changes to the MDM enrollment process. Details about these new features will be public when iOS 7 is released in the fall 2013.

Results of the MDM revolution

There's no doubt that 2010 was *the* important year for MDM, as it was 2010's iOS 4 and Android 2.2 that finally enabled these devices to be manageable. (As you'll see in the next few chapters, the whole story of MDM is much more complicated than that, but nevertheless, 2010 was a watershed year!)

Perhaps the biggest result of the 2010-era changes to iOS and Android was that many people believed that all the problems around BYOD and consumerization would finally be solved. And why wouldn't anyone think so? After all, MDM meant that iPhones and Android devices finally had all of the same hooks and features (more or less) that BlackBerrys had had for years. No more lack of management, so problem solved, right?

Well, maybe not.

As we know now looking back on it, not only did the iPhone and Android mean that users forced new devices into companies, we also had the general "consumerization of IT" movement, which meant that users also moved on to new ways of working. So 2010's management improvements to iOS and Android, while a great first step, were a bit too late to actually solve all of our problems.

We'll take a thorough look at the issues brought up by these changes in Chapter 5, but first we have to dig deeper to the architecture of iOS and Android (Chapter 3) and how MDM works under the hood (Chapter 4).

3. Understanding iOS and Android (From the Enterprise Perspective)

In this book we're focusing primarily on managing Android and iOS devices. Before we can dig into those details, we have to take a closer look at the mobile OSes themselves and how mobile apps actually work.

All About iOS and Android Operating Systems

The important thing to remember is that in many ways, we in the mobile space are very well off. Managing mobile devices is much simpler than managing the other endpoints that IT has been dealing with for years: Windows desktops.

Managing desktops, and specifically Windows, is a huge pain. Windows is well over two decades old, and the business environment that Windows NT was born into in the early 1990s was very different from today's. Back then, the dominance of Windows was far from assured, and one of the techniques Microsoft used to encourage development on the platform was to allow developers to do whatever they wanted. This meant things like giving applications direct access to hardware, letting them store files and make changes wherever they wanted to, and generally letting applications run wild.

The IT world has been paying the price ever since. This relaxed attitude has meant that Windows applications can conflict with each other or break each other (or even break the entire operating system). And even installing applications is hard. You can't just transfer a file and install with one click—instead you have to go through each application's crazy installation routine. Of course we've had two decades to figure out how to solve all these problems, but regardless, managing Windows isn't simple.

What does all this have to do with mobile devices? At first glance, nothing, right? I mean managing the BlackBerrys was always just something the email team did, or maybe there was a "phone person." It was a totally different area from managing desktops.

But (as you're well aware) corporate end-user computing today is just as much about mobile devices as it is about Windows. In the past, access to corporate data was limited to big beige desktops, and then laptops, and finally web apps. Mobile devices back then were limited to pretty much just email. But now they've become elevated to the level of full computers, and as such, the "desktop" people in IT departments now have to deal with mobile devices as well.

Mobile devices are very different from desktops

Since mobile devices are becoming equally as important as desktops for end-user computing, you might be worried that they might be just as difficult to manage. (After all, we've been burned in this way before. Remember when web apps promised to "revolutionize" IT, but then we got mired in security and browser and plug-in compatibility issues?)

But in the mobile world, we're in a good place right now. I can't count the number of experienced desktop admins who marvel at how much simpler and easier mobile OSes are to deal with as compared with full desktop OSes. (That's not a knock on desktop OSes—it's just that each is a product of its time.)

Because mobile OSes are relatively young, the challenges they were built to face are still pretty close to the challenges we have currently, and as a result, we have a much easier time managing mobile devices today than in the crazy world of Windows and Windows applications. For example:

- Android and iOS are user-based operating systems with sandboxed applications. Most processes run with as few permissions as necessary to perform their task, and most apps don't have root access. It's pretty hard for one app to mess with another app, or for an app to mess with the core of the operating system.
- Android and iOS are much closer to being "stateless" operating systems. All settings and configurations are stored in the user area. You can perform an OS upgrade without worrying about screwing everything up, and if a user restores from backup, then everything is right there, instantly.
- Android and iOS have many security features that are natively part of the OS, instead of bolted on as an afterthought.
- Android and iOS have restrictions around application signing and distribution.
- Android and iOS applications can be cleanly installed and removed with ease.

In general, we're talking about a completely different world than what we've dealt with before, and that should make you excited about mobile. (Of course we have other new challenges, but I'll get to those in Chapter 5.)

But not all mobile OSes are the same...

Even though I just talked about how modern mobile OSes—as a group—differ from desktop OSes, I don't want to imply that all modern OSes are the same. In fact, there are quite a few major differences between various mobile operating systems, with the biggest being how they are distributed.

iOS is a closed-source operating system that only comes bundled on Apple iPhones, iPads, and iPod Touches. (iOS is also used for Apple TV, but that version has a different UI and doesn't support third-party apps or MDM at this time, so I'm going to ignore it in this book.) iOS cannot be modified by users or any other third parties, and it cannot be installed onto non-Apple devices.

In contrast, Android is an open-source operating system. It was created as a version of Linux—which is itself an open-source operating system—and it can be freely distributed and modified. It was always the intention that Android would be customized by device manufacturers, and so the reality today is that there are different versions of Android for different devices and manufacturers, each with different capabilities in use, creating market fragmentation. (And headaches for those of us who have to support it!)

Of course there are also plenty of other differences between the two—some of which matter in the context of enterprise mobility and some of which don't—so I'll point them out as they come up.

More mobile OS concepts

Aside from the sandboxing and modernity mentioned before, there are a variety of other mobile OS concepts and components that are relevant to enterprise management, including:

- Software frameworks
- App-to-app interaction
- Permissions
- Multitasking
- Notifications

• Operating system integrity

Software frameworks

Both Android and iOS use software frameworks and built-in applications to provide third-party apps with a wide variety of resources. These system-provided resources mean that individual app developers don't have to reinvent the wheel for common tasks, data can be shared between apps, and the user experience is similar across different apps. (For example, all apps can use the same address book and email UI—whether it's a camera app emailing a picture, a document editor sending a file, or app sending an email—and the experience is the same each time.)

Here are just a few examples of resources that mobile OSes can provide to applications:

• Network access
• Access to hardware (camera, microphone, accelerometer, etc.)
• Access to user data that may be shared (contact lists, calendars, photo albums, email accounts)
• Access for apps to send and receive text messages, dial the phone, or send emails
• GPS and location information
• Storage for app data and settings (This can take place off of the device; an example is Apple's iCloud. This also allows settings and data to be synced to other devices and services.)
• UI elements
• Notifications, both local and from remote servers
• Browsers and rendering engines
• Support for working with audio and video

App-to-app interaction

Since applications are sandboxed from each other and from the operating system, they can't just directly use each other's resources or read each other's files. Instead, the operating system provides strictly controlled and well-defined ways for apps to communicate with each other.

Shared software frameworks and apps provided by the OS comprise one of the main techniques for app interaction. There are frameworks for passing sharing documents directly between apps—for example, iOS's "Open in" function—and there are frameworks that can be used to share data indirectly. For example, a camera app puts a photo in the device's photo album where a social media app could later take that photo from the album and upload it to a website. Once the camera app puts the photo in the album, it becomes a shared resource—the camera app no longer has control of the photo. The clipboard is another example of a shared resource provided by the system. Text can be copied from one app, stored on the device's clipboard while the user opens another app, and then pasted into a text field.

iOS and Android also have ways for apps to communicate directly with each other by creating "ad hoc" relationships. The details of that are beyond the scope of this book, but it will suffice to say that it's generally considered that Android is more flexible and iOS is more tightly controlled when it comes to these techniques. For example, if an iOS app makes a request to open a link in a web browser, it will always be handled by the built-in browser (Safari), even if there are other browsers installed on the device. Contrast that to Android, where the user can choose from a list of whatever browsers are installed and even set a default. The increased flexibility in Android means there are more cool things that Android apps can do, but there are also more opportunities for things to go wrong when an app intentionally or accidentally does something it's not supposed to. And of course, the opposite can be said of iOS. This is just one of several examples of openness in Android that leads people to think that it's less secure.

Another way that apps can interact with each other in both Android and iOS is if they're signed with the same certificate and ID. In this case, apps can use each other's data directly, without going through one of the techniques described previously.

Permissions

If some of these techniques that apps use to communicate with each other sound risky (for example, when they share contacts, photos, or use location data), that's because they are! This is why the concept of "permission" exists. Any time an application wants to do something that could compromise privacy, cost money (like by sending text messages), or affect the overall device, the app has to ask the end user for permission to do it. There are significant differences between how iOS and Android handle this.

iOS apps have to receive permission from the user in order to access location services, contacts, calendars, reminders, Bluetooth, Facebook accounts, and Twitter accounts. The device will ask the user directly the first few times this comes up. A user can also go into the device settings and turn off these permissions at any time, for any particular app.

In Android, the user is presented with the full list of permissions that an application is requesting before the app is installed. The user can review these requests and then decide whether or not to install the app, but there's no other way to control individual app permissions—you either agree to all of them or you don't install the app. And while it's possible for a user to turn off Wi-Fi, cellular data, or location data for the entire device, doing so means none of the other apps get to use those services either. This lack of granular control is definitely a sore spot for Android.

In the next chapter, I'll talk about an especially important permission that Android apps can ask for: access to the Device Administration API, which is used by apps that want to control security features like password policy, encryption, remote wiping, and other things. Device Administration permissions are unique because they can be enabled or disabled by the user on an app-by-app basis.

Multitasking

Mobile OSes must treat multitasking with special care due to the inherently limited power of mobile devices. In iOS, multitasking for apps was essentially nonexistent before version 4. Starting with iOS 4, it was expanded to a specific set of authorized tasks, including playing music, tracking location, VoIP calls, controlling external accessories, downloading newsstand content, and finishing a defined task in a specific period of time. These restrictions have always been a hindrance to developers (especially for third-party email apps, as we'll see in Chapter 8). This will all change soon, however. Starting with iOS 7, multitasking will be available for all types of apps.

Android background tasks have always been much freer. In fact, in the old days of Android, they were so free that poorly designed apps could take up lots of processing power on the phones, and "task killer" utilities were popular downloads for users. These are anachronistic now, though, as Android's task management has advanced considerably.

Notifications

Given the limitations on mobile OS resources, apps can use notifications as an alternative to long-running background process; notifications prompt an app or the user to do a task. One way to do notifications is to schedule them locally on the device. It's like an app is setting an alarm clock for when it's time to do something, and then it goes to sleep until the alarm goes off.

For tasks that are prompted by external servers, apps can ask the device to listen for push notifications, which are delivered to the device via an always-open Internet connection. Both iOS and Android require that push notifications go through their own platform-specific gateways. That means that developers and administrators can't send push notifications directly to apps on their own; instead, they have to register with Apple or Google and send notifications through those gateways. For iOS, the gateway is the Apple Push Notification Service (APNS), which debuted with iOS 3 in 2009. For Android, apps use the Android Cloud to Device Message (C2DM) service, which came out in 2010. (In 2012, C2DM was expanded and renamed Google Cloud Messaging (GCM)).

Both the APNS and GCM can deliver data to a device, but there are a few differences between them. APNS notifications are limited to 256 bytes, but GCM notifications can be much larger.

Currently, APNS can't wake an app on their own or do anything in the background, and instead user interaction is required to respond to a notification and open the associated app. These restrictions will be removed when iOS 7 is released.

Operating system integrity

Android and iOS both have mechanisms to ensure the integrity of the operating system and device, including restrictions around app sources, root access, and booting to alternative OSes. However, there are some major differences between the two platforms, stemming from the fact that Android is much more open than iOS.

Android allows users to install apps from sources other than the Google Play store, though this capability is turned off by default. (The next section will cover app distribution in depth.) Some Android devices also ship with unlockable bootloaders, giving users the ability to boot to an alternative operating system. (Examples include Google Nexus and other devices aimed at developers.) In these cases, users are protected, as the process of booting to an alternative OS erases all of the previously existing user data. For devices that don't ship with unlockable bootloaders, it's usually still possible to find some other way unlock them, but it takes more effort.

Unlike Android, Apple does not allow sideloading apps from alternative marketplaces or booting to alternative OSes. The process of doing these things (along with gaining root access) is collectively referred to as "jailbreaking," and Apple is constantly attempting to make these practices more difficult. Apple has built mechanisms to ensure a secure boot of the iOS environment, and it also prevents devices from downgrading to older OSes, using older OS updates to downgrade, or saving an update and using it to downgrade a device at a later time. Naturally, the people who want to jailbreak iOS always seem to find ways around these security measures anyway, but the fact is that it's getting harder and harder.

Another big difference between iOS and Android is that Apple makes new versions of iOS available immediately to most devices. In the Android world, most carriers and OEMs rarely, if ever, allow users to upgrade to newer versions of Android. This creates a big incentive for users to bypass controls and install alternative OSes on their own.

In both platforms, root access can generally be gained only by exploiting bugs or vulnerabilities in the operating system. (Some alternative versions of Android include root access as a feature of the OS.) But once this happens, all bets are off and security restrictions can be rendered null. In the corporate world, this is a big deal because a jailbroken or rooted mobile device might not respect the standard sandboxing or security rules of an OS and threaten corporate data. (For example, a user who roots his phone might be susceptible to a malicious application that records keystrokes and screenshots and sends them to potential attackers.) I'll cover jailbreaking and rooting more in Chapter 5.

Mobile App Distribution

Besides the mobile OSes themselves, the app distribution ecosystems for iOS and Android are completely different from the way that desktops have traditionally worked. This impacts app distribution, security, development, and management.

iOS app distribution

Any apps that are installed onto iOS devices have to be signed, (even if they're internal apps created by a company). iOS apps can be signed and distributed in several different ways:

- The Apple iOS App Store
- Ad hoc developer distribution
- Enterprise distribution
- The Apple Volume Purchase Program
- The Apple Custom B2B Program

In general, it's very difficult to get unsigned code or apps from other sources to run. Alternative iOS app sources do exist (Cydia, for example), but running those apps requires exploiting some sort of vulnerability to jailbreak the device.

The Apple iOS App Store

Apps that are distributed through the Apple iOS App Store have two main security points going for them. First, the apps go through a quality review process, and second, the identity of app developers is known by Apple, and Apple can revoke any apps at any time.

It wasn't until 2010, two years after the App Store had begun operating, that Apple finally published App Store Review Guidelines. Most of the guidelines are fairly straightforward—apps have to be stable, they have to be free of bugs, and they have to behave in ways that are predictable and don't try to trick the user; apps also have to respect the sandboxing of the OS and may not use unpublished APIs; and apps have to respect the content rating system and can't promote illegal activities. This also included the "we don't need any more fart apps" guideline (Google it).

There are all sorts of stories out there about people having problems with the review guidelines, but for the most part, thousands of businesses and millions of users get their work done every day using apps that are subject to Apple's regulations. That's not to say there aren't the occasional hiccups: Unforeseen delays in the approval process can hinder businesses launching products, and there's no way to easily roll back a buggy app update, which can be a huge problem if your business depends on a particular app. Also, don't forget that Apple takes a 30% cut of paid applications.

Assuming the approval process is successful, Apple signs applications for distribution. Apple can always pull the app from the store, and it can also remotely disable apps. It sounds a bit scary, but ostensibly it's to keep us safe from malware or rogue developers.

The iOS Developer Program

App development is beyond the scope of this book, but it's worth mentioning the ad hoc distribution method. An ad hoc distribution is used when a developer wants to be able to run apps on a small number of devices for testing purposes. (Developers can also use Xcode, Apple's development platform, to run an app on an iOS device that's plugged in with a USB cable.) In order to do an ad hoc distribution, the developer must give Apple a list of device IDs that are to be part of the trial, and then Apple gives the developer a certificate that can be used to sign distribution profiles. The distribution profiles essentially say, "This app has permission to run on these particular devices, and it's signed by this individual developer." People testing the app have to use iTunes to install the provisioning profile and the app itself (or it can be done for them using the iPhone Configuration Utility), and the distribution is limited to 100 devices.

The iOS Developer Enterprise Program

This is the program that IT cares about because this is how companies sign and distribute to their own employees apps they've built internally. (And that's a big distinction—companies are limited to deploying their apps to their own employees. If they want to deploy to other people, they have to use the public Apple App Store and are required to get approval for their apps just like everyone else.)

In order to use the iOS Developer Enterprise Program, the company has to have a DUNS number and pay Apple $299 per year. The DUNS number is a way that Apple can ensure that the company distributing apps is a "real" company and not some random person or scammer with a made-up company using the certificates to distribute apps outside of the controls of the App Store.

Enterprise certificates are also often used to sign custom apps created for companies by outside software developers. Instead of distributing an app in the App Store, a software developer can give the unsigned app directly to the company it developed the app for, allowing the client company to sign it with its own enterprise certificate. This gives a lot more flexibility around licensing and rolling back app editions, and in general makes for a far more enterprise-like scenario than dealing with buying apps in the App Store.

Companies that are part of the iOS Developer Enterprise Program can manually install their apps on iOS devices via iTunes, the iPhone Configuration Utility, or Apple Configurator, or they can distribute them wirelessly (described in Chapter 4). Even though enterprise-signed apps don't go through the public App Store review process, Apple still has the ability to prevent them from running. There are two potential reasons for this: First, a company could violate the terms of the program by distributing apps to non-employees (with contractors and subsidiaries, you can see how this could get murky) or a company could build an app that behaves in a way that Apple doesn't approve of. Now there's not really any way for Apple to actually figure this out, and as far as anybody can tell, this hasn't actually happened. But it's important to note that technically Apple could disable private enterprise iOS apps. Sometimes this makes people uneasy, but like I said earlier, there are thousands of companies out there with thousands of apps that are getting along just fine.

Apple Volume Purchase Program

The Apple Volume Purchase Program (VPP) is another one of those "good to have but not groundbreaking" enterprise mobility offerings. When a company wants to buy lots of copies of a publicly available app for its employees, it can do so in bulk. Apple gives the company a list of redemption codes (along with URLs for convenience), and then distribution of the codes or URLs is up to the company. (Many EMM products can keep track of the codes or URLs automatically.)

Right now, the VPP is available only in a few countries, and there's no way for companies to "take back" a redemption code after it's used unless the device is supervised by the Apple Configurator. (See Chapter 4 to learn about the Apple Configurator.) So while the VPP is convenient, it's still not quite like "real" software licensing.

Apple Custom B2B program

Companies can use Apple's Custom B2B program to purchase and distribute one of a kind apps from developers. The program uses the infrastructure of the Apple App Store and the VPP to handle distribution, so that means apps are subject to the App Store approval process, and you still have the same limitations around regaining licenses and international support.

Android app distribution

Just like iOS apps, all Android apps must be signed, but the similarities end there. In Android, anyone can sign an app and distribute it in any way he likes, which makes the ecosystem much more open. Most people think of the Google Play store as the Android version of the Apple App Store, and certainly the Google Play store is the primary curated app marketplace for Android apps, but it's important to point out that Android developers don't have to use the Google Play store. It's just an option for them.

While the general feel in the industry is that it's easier for malware and low-quality apps to get into Google Play than the Apple App store, Android developers submitting to Google Play do have to abide by certain policies, which—similar to those for iOS—protect from offensive or illegal content, explicit material, and apps that exhibit deceptive behavior. In February 2012, Google announced it had been using a service called Bouncer for several months, and that Bouncer analyzes new and existing applications to check for malware and viruses. It's reasonable to consider that users who stick to the Google Play store will be fairly safe, and Google points out that most of the malware and viruses in the Android ecosystem come from sources outside of Google Play.

Apps that are distributed outside of Google Play are referred to as apps from "non-market sources," and users have to change a setting on their device in order to install these apps. These app sources include carriers, OEMs, general alternative marketplaces, corporate-deployed apps, random websites, and really just anyone else that wants to build or distribute an app. With Android, the OEM customization process means that some users might not be allowed to install non-market apps, or the device might be locked into another alternative app store. Some alternative app sources might be well curated and secure, while others could easily contain malware. This can be confusing for users at companies that deploy in-house apps, because while they might want to just play it safe and stick with Google Play, installing corporate-deployed apps means installing apps from non-market sources.

4. Understanding Mobile Device Management

Now that we've covered the basics of mobile OSes and apps, we can dig into how these things are managed. As I've mentioned several times, the general concept of managing mobile devices is called (wait for it...) mobile device management, often shortened to MDM. MDM is not the name of any one product from any particular vendor, but rather it's the general name of the category of products that vendors sell to manage mobile devices. ("Mobile devices" in this case are defined as devices that run mobile OSes, like iOS, Android, Windows Phone, Symbian, BlackBerry OS, etc.)

MDM Concepts

To use MDM software to manage a mobile device, you need three main components:

- You need a device that has the ability to be managed—that is, it has to have some way to remotely configure settings, execute management actions, and query for information.
- You need an over-the-air network connection to the device.
- You need some kind of management server or service where you can configure management policies that you'll push out to the mobile devices you're managing.

Let's take a look at each one of these in a bit more detail.

Device settings, actions, and information

Provisioning a device for corporate use usually means configuring various device features. This could entail enabling encryption and passwords, setting up Wi-Fi or VPN access, configuring email accounts, or changing any other security-type settings. (You can read all about the specifics later when we discuss each platform in detail.)

Aside from applying initial settings, you can also take direct management actions on a device, like installing and removing applications, wiping the device, or setting a password.

The final part is to query the device itself for information. This means finding out the device's location, what apps are installed on it, identifying information about the device (model, phone number, serial number, IMEI, etc.), the state of the hardware (battery level, available storage, etc.), or anything else that a user is doing to the device.

Over-the-air management

Many of the settings that IT cares about need to be configured only once, when a device is first provisioned. After that, they might not ever change. But since mobile devices are...well...mobile, there are also a lot of things that are more effective to do over there air. Sure, you can wipe a device by going into the settings menu and finding the appropriate commands, but what good does that do you when the user left his phone in a taxi? So really, it's the over-the-air remote management that enables policies to actually be effective. Otherwise, you're just hoping the users don't change them or that nothing unpredictable happens.

These over-the-air management capabilities are then used to plug the device into some sort of service, and then there you have it—that's mobile device management as we know it! This service that you use to change settings over the air can be a cloud service or an on-premises server. But once you have it, you have the ability to set up a device, take actions, and learn information about it, all wirelessly and over the air.

This goes to show why the features added to iOS and Android 2010 were so important. iOS 4 meant that configuration profiles could be managed over the air, and Android 2.2's Device Administration API meant that device-wide security settings were actually exposed to administrators for the first time.

Having said this, it's important to note that there are forms of MDM that don't use over-the-air management. We'll learn about these later, and they include supervised devices with the Apple Configurator or certain uses of the iPhone Configuration Utility.

Policy services

Once you have a device that can be managed and an over-the-air connection to do it remotely, the final step is to have a server on the other end to do the actual management. You always do the basics manually—configure settings, execute management actions, and query for device information—but the real power comes from building policies that can automate and scale common tasks.

MDM servers can use logic to build policies that combine device queries, management actions, and settings to accomplish tasks that go way beyond just pushing a few management buttons. Most MDM servers not only have policies for common tasks already built in, but also allow you to build your own policies. Policies can also get more powerful by going beyond the device and incorporating management tasks and sources of information from other enterprise management systems.

Exchange ActiveSync as MDM

You probably know about Microsoft Exchange ActiveSync (EAS) as pretty much the de facto standard for mobile email syncing these days. But did you also know that EAS is valuable as an MDM tool? EAS has the advantage that it's supported by many different devices (remember that it was the only way to manage an iPhone over the air until iOS 4), it does the basics of MDM, and it's probably already available in your environment for free. (Well, "free" if you're using Exchange.)

There are a few catches, though. First, when I say EAS provides only the basics of MDM, I really mean it. It's very bare-bones compared with the third-party MDM solutions covered later in this chapter.

Second, EAS doesn't always have the ability to manage the entire mobile device—it's really more like "email client management" than mobile device management, as EAS specifies and enforces policies for the users' email clients. The good news is that most of the time, users sync their email via the client that's built into the operating system, and with these built-in clients management policies get passed through and applied to the entire device.

But it's also possible to sync EAS connections to third-party freestanding apps on the mobile devices. (There are third-party email clients in the app stores, for example.) In these cases, while the actual email app will respect your EAS management policies, it won't pass anything through to the device itself. So for example, say you want to use EAS to make sure that all of your users' devices are protected with eight-digit passwords. Most of your users are probably using the mail clients that are built into their phones, so they'll have the eight-digit passwords on their devices. However, some of them could go to an app store and download a third-party EAS client app. When email is synced to that app, it will have to respect the eight-digit password requirement, but that password requirement won't apply to the entire device. That user will still be walking around with a wide-open phone. If that policy was created in hopes that it would protect all the devices, then it has failed.

You're probably thinking that this sounds bad, because it means EAS is not really MDM, right? (Even though Microsoft calls it MDM...) Fortunately, there are two reasons why things aren't all that bad. First, even though the device in the example above wouldn't have a password, the third-party app still does, so at least email would still be protected by policy. (Remember, EAS should be thought of as "email client management," not "device management.") Second, thanks to policies available in Exchange, administrators are able to know what clients are being used to sync mail, and can set policies to block or allow different ones. (So you can actually entirely block EAS syncing for users who aren't using the built-in clients—well, assuming they haven't jailbroken their phones! More on that later in the book though...) For now, let's look at EAS management a bit more.

EAS management

When you first start looking into EAS policies, you might get excited about its potential as a "real" MDM tool because there are all these settings in there about blacklisting and whitelisting third-party apps, blocking unsigned apps, preventing tethering, and all this other device-level stuff. Don't get too excited though, because those are just old policies left over from the Windows Mobile days from the past decade—most of today's email clients will completely ignore them.

However, there are still plenty of other basic policies that will work with today's EAS clients (remember that the "client" can be a device or an app), including the ability to configure settings for all sorts of different password policies, encryption, use of the camera and the browser, and SSL message encryption. The possible management actions are remote-wiping the entire client or simply de-provisioning the EAS connection. Last, EAS can also query the client for identifying information like the client or device ID, model, and OS.

On the server and policy side, EAS can block connections from any client that isn't able to respect the management settings. (These are referred to as non-provisionable devices.) So, for instance, you could block EAS syncing to clients that don't support encryption.

A downside of EAS is that client management policies are actually determined on a per-mailbox basis, rather than a per-device basis. So essentially each user gets just one set of security policies for all their clients. This can be a problem if a user has two different clients that require two different levels of security.

Fortunately, things are more granular when it comes to determining what devices have access to email in the first place. Starting with Exchange 2010 SP2, the client access rules became granular enough to block or control access from individual devices or clients, not just based on the device model as was previously the case.

What's missing from EAS management

The problem with EAS is that there are many aspects of a device that it cannot address. This is probably best illustrated by looking at the long list of things that third-party MDM solutions (which I'll dig into in the next section) can do that EAS can't do, including:

- The ability to have knowledge about what apps on the devices.
- Anything having to do with location.
- The ability to deploy Wi-Fi or VPN settings.
- The ability to provision Exchange accounts over the air.
- The ability to work with devices that don't have an Exchange account associated with them.

As I mentioned before, there's also the issue that sometimes the EAS client can be the user's whole device (so you know you're protecting it) and sometimes the EAS client can be just an app (where you're not able to apply policies to the device). Fortunately, there are ways of dealing with this. Remember that EAS does return information about the client—so you can tell whether your policies are being applied to a user's entire device or just a third-party app. And then you can also use the client access rules discussed above to block third-party apps from syncing, so that if users want email on their devices at all, they have to use the built-in app. Of course, they can still opt out of that and just not have email on their devices, but it's pretty much that way with all MDM—users have to opt in, and when they do, they get both corporate data and management policies.

The bottom line with EAS management is that you'll be able to protect email with a few basic policies, and you can determine what clients are allowed to have access in the first place. The bigger problems arise when you realize that EAS doesn't give you any visibility into anything else that's happening on the device. This is important because there are a lot of other things that a device (or apps installed on a device) could do to data contained in the email. To have more visibility, you need to go to full-scale "real" MDM, which we'll look at now.

MDM for iOS

Let's look at how this full-scale MDM works for iOS, and then after that we'll look at how it works for Android.

MDM for iOS revolves around the notion of "configuration profiles"—XML files installed onto the device that contain instructions for modifying and controlling settings. Recall that while configuration profiles were introduced with iPhone OS 2 back in 2008, they got interesting for MDM purposes in 2010 with iOS 4. The big change in 2010 was that these configuration profiles could be installed and managed wirelessly over the air—before that, you had to plug an iPhone into a computer via USB to apply a profile. The other big change in 2010 was that these configuration profiles could enable a wider range of over-the-air management tasks than what was available with EAS (the only option for over-the-air management before 2010).

iOS configuration profiles can be created using utilities from Apple, which include the iPhone Configuration Utility and the Apple Configurator; they can be created by third-party MDM services; or (if you're hard core) you can even write the XML files from scratch. From there, there are several methods to get the profile (the XML file) to the device: via USB using one of the desktop utilities, by sending the file via email or having the user download it from a website, or through wireless enrollment protocols via MDM servers.

iOS configuration profile contents

iOS configuration profiles are split up into different groups of settings, called "payloads," which are all listed below. When profiles are distributed or modified, you can work with just individual payloads or send groups of them. Devices can handle multiple payloads in the same category—for example, you could give a user sets of Wi-Fi credentials for multiple networks that would each be a separate payload. It's also possible to install profiles from different sources, though a device can be linked to only one MDM server at a time (through the "mobile device management" payload).

Here's the full list of the payloads and what they do:

General settings

Contains the name, description, and identifier of the profile itself, as well as settings that determine whether or not a profile can be removed or if it needs a password to be removed. (The catch is that profiles can only be locked on to devices when they're installed via USB.) It can also have a description of the profile to show to the users.

Passcode policy

These all have to do with passcode complexity, with policies for age, numeric values, length, reuse, and device locking. There's also an option to auto-wipe the device after a certain number of failed attempts.

Restrictions

There are many features in here that change how a device works and what the user experience will be like. These include preventing a user from installing apps; blocking the camera, FaceTime, screenshots, Siri, voice dialing, gaming, YouTube, iTunes, Safari, and iCloud; forcing backups to be encrypted; and content ratings for iTunes and the App Store. Basically, it's all the stuff that can make an iPhone less fun.

Wi-Fi

This contains all the information to automatically set up a user's Wi-Fi access.

VPN

All of the settings for installing device-wide virtual private networks; it supports several popular VPN providers.

Email

Settings for IMAP and POP email accounts.

Exchange ActiveSync

Settings for corporate EAS accounts. Important settings include SSL requirements, the ability to prevent users from forwarding emails from one account using another account, and the ability to prevent third-party apps from sending emails using the EAS account

LDAP, CalDAV, CardDAV, Subscribed Calendars

If your company uses any of these, credentials can be added here and they'll show up in the calendar, contacts, and email apps.

Web Clips

These create links to URLs, and unlike apps, they can be silently pushed and removed. They can also be made nonremovable, and the address bar can be hidden.

Credentials

Can add X.509 certificates to authenticate a device to various enterprise services, or for encryption and authentication of the profile itself.

SCEP

Settings for SCEP (Simple Certificate Enrollment Protocol), a scheme that can be used to verify device identity information, enroll devices in MDM, and deliver encrypted profiles to devices.

Mobile Device Management

This is the important payload, because it contains credentials to wirelessly link devices to management services. The options for the MDM payload include URLs for the MDM server, authentication credentials, information about Apple Push Notification Service (APNS), whether management commands should be signed, and whether the device should notify the server when the profile is removed.

Aside from making the MDM connection itself, this payload specifies what you (as the administrator) can actually do to the device.

The first group of settings gives permission to query the device for general settings, security settings, network settings, restrictions, configuration profiles, applications, and provisioning profiles. Next are the direct management actions: adding and removing configuration profiles, provisioning profiles, apps (special note—and this is a big one—MDM cannot remove apps installed by users), and settings (i.e., all of the other settings in configuration profiles). The last subgroup gives permission to change the device password or remote-wipe the device.

Keep in mind that you can use configuration profiles without using the mobile device management payload—you just won't be able to do anything to the profiles or the device over the air.

APN (Access Point Name)

These settings are related to how the device connects to carrier 3G and 4G data networks. They don't really get used in most MDM situations.

Tools from Apple

Apple provides several tools for working with iOS devices, including:

- iPhone Configuration Utility
- iTunes
- Apple Configurator

iPhone Configuration Utility

The iPhone Configuration Utility is a free desktop application from Apple (available for OS X and Windows) that's used for working with iOS configuration profiles, provisioning profiles, apps, and devices. Profiles created with the utility can be installed directly via USB, installed via email, or hosted on a web page so users can download them. The utility can also be used to install enterprise apps directly, find out information about devices, and export logs (for app development purposes).

The great thing about the iPhone Configuration Utility is that it gives you all the exact same device-level functionality that's available to any MDM provider. If you want to be an expert on iOS MDM, start playing with the Configuration Utility! You can essentially perform all of the same configurations, queries, and management actions that any MDM solution can do. (It's just that you won't be able to do it over the air, since you need an MDM server to do that.)

iTunes

While iTunes isn't usually considered a mobile device management tool, it can be used for certain tasks that aren't possible with MDM. The most substantial capabilities are that iTunes can back up iOS devices; activate, update, and restore devices; and sync iTunes media. iTunes can also be used to install and rearrange apps, and file-sharing apps can opt to use iTunes as a method for transferring documents between the app and a computer. While many of these tasks can be accomplished with iCloud and there's no real need to use iTunes in this capacity these days, iCloud has been criticized for its instability and iTunes remains an attractive alternative.

When it comes to controlling device backups, it's possible to use MDM to prevent users from backing up a device to iCloud. It is not possible, though, to prevent a user from backing up a device to iTunes, but you can still require that any iTunes backups be encrypted and password-protected.

What's in an iOS backup? Basically everything except for the actual apps themselves, iTunes media, and mail messages. So that means contacts and email settings that were entered by the user, call logs, text messages, all the photos in the camera roll, lists of what apps are on the device, browsing history, bookmarks, or anything else that was set up by a user. (iTunes takes care of storing the media and the actual apps, and email accounts on the email servers store the user's messages.) This backup can be used to configure new devices with existing settings, and it's also possible to take a backup and use it as a "golden image" to configure additional devices.

Backups also include any configuration profiles the where installed on the device, which means that the backup can contain corporate credentials and other data. While a backup from one device can be installed on another device, configuration profiles that are part of a backup will be restored only to the original device.

Apple Configurator

The Apple Configurator is a Mac OS X application from Apple that's used to manage iOS devices. You can think of it as combining some features of iTunes with features from the iPhone Configuration Utility. It can manage iOS backups as well as configuration profiles, apps, and devices. The catch is that most of the management tasks require the devices to be plugged in via USB, and then they're tied to the same computer for any subsequent management. (And that computer has to be a Mac, since the Apple Configurator doesn't exist for Windows.)

The Apple Configurator has three sets of functions, called Prepare, Supervise, and Assign.

Using the "Prepare" function, you can install configuration profiles and apps, create backups, install backups, and update iOS. (This requires the device to be physically connected.) Another interesting feature is you can set up an iOS device with all the apps, settings, profiles, and other information you want, create a backup of that device, and then use the backup as a golden image to install on other devices.

The "Supervise" function lets you lock down a device to a greater degree than is possible with configuration profiles installed over the air. The additional management techniques include:

- More options for the Restrictions configuration profile payload, including blocking iMessage, configuring the Siri profanity filter, blocking the Bookstore app and erotica within Bookstore, preventing the user from removing apps, preventing the installation of other configuration profiles, and blocking the Game Center app.
- Installing a configuration profile payload for a global HTTP proxy.
- Locking the device down to a single app so that you can't go back to the home screen.
- Setting the lock-screen background and lock-screen welcome message.

It's possible to use the Supervise function as a one-time device setup tool to get the expanded configuration options. The devices have to be connected by USB to do the initial setup, but then if you include MDM server credentials in the configuration profile, the device and profiles can subsequently be managed over the air. You can also use the Supervise function to refresh devices by connecting to the Apple Configurator.

Last, the "Assign" function lets you manage users' iOS images separately from devices. This way you can have more users than devices, and check images in and out as needed. This is often used in schools where multiple classes share one set of iPads.

iOS MDM: Putting it all together

All of these tools from Apple are great for doing their specific management tasks, but as discussed in Chapter 3, the important aspect of MDM is making an over-the-air connection to a remote management server. Once that connection is made, the MDM server configures the device and takes management actions as needed, either through direct commands by administrators or through automated policies.

The first task for MDM is enrolling devices. To do this, you have to figure out how to deliver to the device a profile with credentials for the management server (contained in the mobile device management payload). You can always just email the profile, host it on a website, or install it via USB. However, profiles often contain sensitive, personalized information like email credentials, so you want to be sure of the identity of the device and the user before you let those be installed.

To do this, iOS can use something called SCEP (Simple Certificate Enrollment Protocol) to ensure that profiles delivered over the air are encrypted and can only be installed by the correct user on a the correct device. Most MDM solutions handle all of this for you, but here's what's going on:

First, a user logs into a web portal provided by the MDM server. The link to the web portal can be provided via text message, email, or web link, or be embedded in an app. After logging in, the MDM server sends an initial profile to the device. The user accepts the profile, and once it's installed, the device sends identifying information about the device back to the server.

Once the server has that information, it sends another profile containing a SCEP payload. The SCEP payload contains information that the device uses to acquire a certificate from the certificate authority associated with the MDM server. After that certificate is installed, the device can then receive encrypted profiles from the MDM server that contain further configuration instructions.

Keep in mind that any time a profile is installed on a device, it warns the user that the device can be remotely managed and that settings can be changed, and it asks for permission to proceed.

This way any time over-the-air management is involved, the user always has to consent and opt in or out.

Once a profile is installed, in order to make changes and initiate management actions on the device, the MDM server contacts the device using the Apple Push Notification Service. This prompts the device to check with the server to see if there are any changes. The MDM server can:

- Query the device for information
- Add or remove profiles
- Add or remove apps
- Turn off voice and data roaming
- Remote lock, wipe, or clear the password

The over-the-air MDM relationship can be severed at any time by either party. The user can remove configuration profiles, the MDM server can remove profiles, or profiles can be made to expire on their own. When a profile is removed, any settings, applications, provisioning profiles, and certificates that were installed as part of a profile are removed as well. This means that any credentials or apps deployed by profiles and used to access sensitive information will also be removed.

You might have noticed that some iOS MDM products use agent applications, but none of the techniques we talked about so far require an app. So what does an MDM agent app do? MDM vendors typically use agent apps to provide shortcuts to MDM enrollment URLs. They can also be used to attempt to find out if the device is jailbroken or to collect location information—things that profiles can't access, but apps can. This data can be reported back to the MDM server and incorporated into management policies.

How iOS MDM controls applications

Now let's take a closer look at how these MDM products interact with apps themselves. There are three basic ways MDM can interact with apps:

- MDM can install and remove apps from the Apple App Store.

- MDM can install and remove apps signed using the iOS Developer Enterprise Program.
- MDM can be aware of apps that users install on their own (but it can't do anything directly to those apps).

Looking at each of these:

Managing public apps from the Apple App Store

An MDM server that's linked to a device can command it to install publicly available apps from the Apple App Store. The user must acknowledge and accept the installation, and the user can remove these apps at any time (unless the device is managed in Supervise mode with the Apple Configurator). Using MDM, these apps can be prevented from being backed up to iTunes or iCloud, they can be removed any time, and finally, like other configuration profile-related settings, they can be set to be removed when the device is unenrolled from management.

Corporate-signed apps

Remember that companies can use the iOS Developer Enterprise Program to sign in-house apps created for their own employees. An MDM server can manage these apps in the same way as managed public apps described above. It's also possible to install corporate-signed apps on devices that aren't managed by MDM, but in this case, it won't be possible for IT to remove these apps, so the apps should have other authorization or security mechanisms if they contain sensitive corporate data.

Reporting on user-installed apps

One of the weak points for iOS MDM (depending on your point of view) is that over-the-air management doesn't have any direct way of controlling apps that users install on their own. There may be situations where you don't want certain apps to be installed on the same devices that are used to access corporate resources. Unfortunately, there's simply no part of the configuration profile or MDM that allows you to blacklist individual apps from the Apple App Store or remove user-installed apps.

To solve this, you have to use an MDM server policy that takes advantage of the queries, and management actions are available to build a policy that, to some degree or another, accomplishes a similar goal. In this case, the server could query a device to see what applications a user has installed. When the server finds a blacklisted app, it can send a notification of noncompliance to the user, asking that the offending app be removed. If the user doesn't comply, the MDM server can respond by removing his Exchange account, removing corporate apps, or taking some other punitive action.

This "badger the user into compliance" technique may not be elegant, but at least it provides a way (albeit indirect) to prevent the blacklisted application from being present on the same device as corporate data.

New iOS 7 features

Don't forget that some aspects of MDM and configuration profiles will change when iOS 7 is released in the fall 2013. I can't write about those new changes yet because they're covered by a nondisclosure agreement, and I don't want to just speculate, either. What I can do is list the features that Apple hinted at during the 2013 Worldwide Developers Conference keynote:

- Per-app VPN.
- Improvements for app licensing and the Volume Purchase Program.
- Wireless app configuration and managed app configuration.
- Enterprise single sign-on.
- Default data protection for third-party apps.
- Streamlined MDM enrollment.

MDM for Android

Despite all the limitations in iOS management, at least it has well-defined configuration profiles that are the same for every device. When it comes to Android, almost every device model and every single vendor has slightly different capabilities. As a consequence, if you want to manage different types of Android devices, you can usually rely on only a minimum set of capabilities that's common to them all. Let's look at how Android management came to this and whether it's really as bad as it seems.

Remember that when Android was created, it was intended to be just a basic starting point operating system that mobile device manufacturers could easily customize for their own devices. The core version of Android didn't have any management APIs, as it was assumed the OEMs would add them. But in the rush to get Android devices to market, many vendors didn't add their own management APIs. Soon enough, it became apparent that it would be useful to have at least some kind of management in the core version of Android, which is what led to the Device Administration API.

Device Administration API

In 2010, version 2.2 of Android introduced the Device Administration API to provide a management framework. It featured controls to:

- Require a device password, and set a minimum length or require an alphanumeric password
- Erase a device after a maximum number of failed unlock attempts
- Automatically lock the device after a maximum period of inactivity
- Remotely lock a device
- Remotely reset the password
- Remotely wipe the device

Android 3.0 added controls to:

- Require more complex policies, including letters, numbers, and special symbols, and to specify the minimum numbers of uppercase and lowercase letters, numbers, and special symbols
- Set the password expiration length and prevent password reuse

- Require device encryption

Android 4.0 added camera controls to the Device Administration API.

Instead of using a configuration profile to interact with these APIs (like in iOS), with Android, any app can interact with them by simply asking the user for Device Administrator permission. (So be wary of the free flashlight app that you sideload that asks for Device Administrator permissions!) Vendors that want to create MDM for Android have to build an app that interacts with these APIs and connects to an external management server.

Other APIs

While the Device Administration API provides some of the core device-level MDM functions for Android, it doesn't provide nearly as many controls as iOS configuration profiles do. So if a vendor builds an Android MDM app that only uses the Device Administration API, they won't get very many features. So what can they do to get more functionality?

For one thing, it turns out that many of the tasks that MDM needs to do can be accomplished with all of the other APIs that are in Android. For example, any random app can ask to use location data or gather other information about the device. On the other hand, there's still a long list of other tasks left over that just aren't possible on basic core Android. This is where the OEMs come in.

With the exception of Google Nexus devices, the implementation of Android on any given device will have all sorts of modifications, which usually include some additional management APIs (beyond the Device Administration API). However, these extra APIs are OEM-specific and not common to all Android devices. The result is that Samsung, Motorola, HTC, and all the other vendors have slightly different MDM capabilities despite the fact that they all run the same OS. Ugh. This is a clear illustration of Android fragmentation and why it's unlikely to ever go away. Sure, it would be nice if all the vendors would create a standard set of management APIs or if the core version of Android could go ahead and have more features, but that doesn't seem to be happening.

On top of all this, most Android devices don't get updated to the most recent versions of the operating system (due in large part to the fact that Android on most devices is highly customized, and device makers would rather focus their efforts on adapting new versions of Android to the newest devices only). It's not uncommon for Android devices—especially the cheap ones—to ship with old versions of Android even when they're brand new. This means that you might not always be able to count on recently introduced APIs being present.

MDM vendors deal with this by trying to make their apps work with as many of the different manufacturers' APIs as possible. It's their goal to be able to make their MDM apps work as consistently as possible across different devices despite the different APIs. That's a tall order, and it also goes to show why Android MDM is much more difficult than iOS MDM.

The reality, though, is that complete consistency is impossible, so many MDM vendors just break out different feature lists for different devices. For example, Samsung has a particularly robust set of custom management APIs marketed as SAFE (which stands for Samsung Approved For Enterprise). So the MDM vendor will say, "Here's what our product can do with typical devices, and here's what we can do with Samsung phones with the SAFE APIs."

What can you do with a "typical" Android device?

Despite all the fragmentation, a lot of people still want to think of Android devices in a generic sense. So if you look at a "typical" device (not counting advanced Samsung SAFE devices or extreme low-end tablets), what do you get?

- passcode enforcement
- software inventory
- storage encryption
- auto-lock after a set time

- app blacklisting/whitelisting
- block settings changes/kiosk mode
- configure EAS in native client
- configure Wi-Fi
- control camera
- detect rooted devices
- remote lock
- remote wipe
- send messages to users
- wipe after a certain number of failed unlock attempts

These features are made possible by a mixture of Device Administration APIs, normal core Android APIs, and custom OEM APIs.

Regardless of what an average device may be like, you still have to deal with the fact that Android MDM won't always be consistent. Also remember that since each MDM vendor has to build its own Android app, there will be some variance between MDM vendors, too. To really know what you can do with Android MDM, you have to go to each individual vendor and find out what features it supports for different devices. (Of course, in the real world, enterprise mobility management is about a lot more than feature comparison matrices.)

One common way to deal with fragmentation is to look at all the capabilities of all the different Android devices in the world and then just sort of draw a line to define the minimum standards you'd like to support. (And to be frank, the enterprise users we worry about likely have decent phones, too, so you probably don't have to worry about supporting low-end, pre-Android 2.2 devices anyway.)

Another solution to all this fragmentation is that since the early days of Android, mobility solutions have made up for MDM shortcomings by implementing some management features in specialized apps instead of dealing with the mess of different device-level capabilities, rendering the underlying Android version less important. This is something I'll explore a lot more later on in the book. By relying less on the operating system for some tasks and setting minimum standards for others, you can achieve a relatively consistent level of functionality.

Other components of Android MDM

It's hard to give a lot of detail about general Android MDM, since everything varies so much. And unlike with iOS, there's no "Android Configuration Utility" or any other universal tools to test MDM features. (So you'll just have to bug MDM vendors for free trials.) That said, we can still look at some basic aspects of MDM and see how they get implemented in Android, keeping in mind that some devices may have additional capabilities beyond these.

Enrolling an Android device in MDM simply involves installing a Device Administration-enabled app that also can make an over-the-air connection to a management server. Users typically authenticate to the server within the app, and the app asks the user for permission to act as a Device Administrator. Once the user gives consent, the app can make changes to device-wide security policies. The app can take care of any subsequent configuration changes, queries, and management actions through further communication with the MDM server. Some MDM apps run constantly in the background, while others use push notifications from the server to wake the app as needed.

When management is no longer desired, the server can remotely disable the app or sever the management connection. Users can also end management by revoking Device Administration permissions in the device settings or by uninstalling the MDM app. (As an interesting note, Android's built-in mail client also uses the Device Administration API. When the user connects to Exchange ActiveSync, it will enforce any associated management policies on the entire device.)

When it comes to apps, Android MDM can't have any direct control over apps that are installed by users (just like with iOS). However, it's still possible to blacklist apps using the roundabout technique I talked about earlier. Both public and corporate apps can be installed on users' devices simply by sending a link to wherever the app is hosted or by just sending the app itself. The user acknowledges that he wants to install the app and is aware of the permissions that it needs to run, and then it will install. (Remember, if the app is a corporate-signed app, users will have to go into the device settings and check the box to allow apps from unknown sources.)

As with all MDM, the server can take device queries and management actions—as well as external queries and actions—and use them to build complex policies. What's interesting about Android is that unlike with iOS configuration profiles, since Android MDM is administered as an actual standalone Android app, MDM vendors can give that app the ability to enforce policies locally without an over-the-air connection to the MDM server. (So the local app can say, "Hey, you just entered a danger zone so I'm turning off your camera," if that rule was set up ahead of time.)

So there you have it! That's an overview of what MDM is and how it works for iOS and Android. Does this solve all of our problems? Read on to find out.

5. The Reality of Mobile Device Management

I spent the past few chapters describing mobile device management technology and how it applies to iOS and Android devices. Now, in this chapter, I'm going to step out of the weeds a bit and talk about MDM in the context of how it applies to users and IT.

We already know that, in general, iOS and Android management wasn't all that great before 2010. The enterprise was dealing with a flood of these devices, with little that could be done to manage them. But then, in 2010, all of the MDM pieces (over-the-air configuration profiles and the Device Administration API) came into place, enabling iPhones and Android phones to be treated just like any other enterprise resources.

Once iPhones and iPads and Android devices are managed and locked down in the same way you manage a desktop or a BlackBerry, all of the problems that come with these mobile devices should disappear, right? After all, IT has been locking down users' mobile devices for a decade, so wouldn't it logically follow that this would work here, too?

Unfortunately, there are some pretty big problems with this idea, not the least of which is that users flat out won't like having a restricted experience. Locking down a device doesn't make the effects of consumerization go away, and in fact, it probably makes things worse by driving users further underground. Not that this really matters, though, because today's MDM technology isn't quite perfect anyway.

I'm not trying to paint a picture that things are all bad for MDM. While the first half of this chapter is going to take a hard look at all of the real-world challenges that MDM faces (both for users and for IT), this doesn't mean I hate MDM. In fact, I love MDM! The second half of this chapter focuses on the places where MDM really shines and is working—right now—for thousands of organizations. I'll finish this chapter by identifying the main reason why enterprise mobility management needs to go beyond just using MDM (which is the second half of this book).

The Reality of MDM for End Users

I keep on talking about how 2010 was a big year for MDM, but think about what 2010 was like from an end user's standpoint. By then, people had been already using iPhones and Android for a couple of years, and in many cases, they'd already brought those phones into their workplaces. Depending on the company, a few different things could have been going on:

- IT could have been ignoring the new devices.
- IT could have been completely unaware of the new devices.
- Because of the new devices, there could have been friction between IT and users.
- iPhones and Android might even have been officially sanctioned by way of Exchange ActiveSync management or third-party sandboxed email clients.

No matter what the situation was, IT had little or no control over iPhones and Android, because for the most part, the technology simply didn't exist. That is, not until 2010! In 2010, IT might even have started rejoicing that it finally had BlackBerry-like management tools for the iPhone and Android called MDM. Yay! But what did it mean for the user experience?

What happens when MDM comes along? Time for a story about a user.

Imagine you're a typical employee of a company in late 2010 or early 2011. Your company's IT department has just been sold MDM software by one of dozens of vendors (both new and old) that are suddenly offering it. Your company executives announce, "Congratulations, everyone, we now have a BYOD program!" Of course you've been using your iPhone at work for a year now, so you wonder what they're talking about and how life is going to be any different from before. You're probably just thinking, "Are they going to start paying my phone bill or something? That'd be cool!" But it's not going to be like that at all.

You find out what this BYOD stuff really means when you come in one day and realize you can no longer get on the Wi-Fi network (which isn't really a problem because your phone has a 3G connection) and you can't get your work email. (More of a problem, though you can still access Outlook Web Access.)

To get back into your company's Wi-Fi and email, your IT department tells you to visit a website to download a configuration profile. You log in , and an iOS configuration profile installs itself on your phone. A few warning screens come up, but you just click "next, next, next, okay, I agree..." just like any of the software installations you've been doing for almost two decades now.

But once that's done, your phone suddenly asks you to set an eight-digit password. And then it tells you that you that social media apps are forbidden and you have to uninstall your Facebook app!

The worst part is that when you're at home that night, your kid grabs your iPhone (as usual, since it's the only thing that keeps him quiet). You forget that it has a long password now. Your kid types away, entering the password incorrectly. It only takes entering the password incorrectly a few times and suddenly your device is wiping itself out.

Needless to say, this is a worst-case scenario that combines all of the common bad MDM experience anecdotes. But it also illustrates the root of the issue: Users' relationships with their iPhones and Android phones are completely different from their relationships with BlackBerrys. iPhones and Android phones—even with MDM—are not the same as BlackBerrys. Attempting to treat them in the same way won't work.

How management needs have changed

As I mentioned before, while iPhones and Android phones were becoming popular, consumers (and thus end users) were also becoming more plugged into technology. Everything was becoming more powerful, more connected, and easier to use, and iPhones and Android phones—with their easy-to-use app stores—were the perfect tools to enable all of this.

Naturally, our users wanted to take advantage of all these great tools to do their jobs. Sure, their work BlackBerrys also had third-party apps, but it just wasn't the same. They wanted iPhones and Android phones. Soon your workplace was full of them, and work data was living on the same devices as personal data.

Make no mistake, this was a dangerous situation. Remember from Chapter 3 that these new mobile OSes were designed to be able to easily share data between different apps. For instance, if someone sends a corporate document to a user's Exchange account that's synced to an iPhone, it can easily be uploaded to Dropbox—an obvious data leak. (And there are many other examples that could be given.)

But then, in 2010, MDM came along! Problem solved? Well, maybe, depending on what your definition of "solved" is. The problem is that MDM has very little control over all this data sharing (or leaking) that goes on between apps. The only way to prevent this type of data leaking is to lock down the user experience for the entire device, because MDM on its own just isn't that granular.

Of course, there are good reasons why IT used MDM to lock down these new phones, not the least of which is the fact that "lock it down" was the attitude that IT had been taking for decades. So it's only natural that when MDM came along, many people thought, "Great, iPhone problem solved!"

Yes, locking down an iPhone does technically solve the problem, but it solved the *old* problem. People don't love their iPhones because they have touchscreens and are made out of metal—they love them because they can do all kinds of fun, awesome, and powerful things. (And this just isn't fun for users' personal lives—it also makes them more productive at work!) So if you try to solve the issue of work stuff and personal stuff intermingling by locking down all the personal stuff, you haven't really solved the problem at all—you've just swept it under the rug. This is why iPhones and Android phones are very different from the old locked-down corporate devices of yesterday.

Another factor that makes managing iPhones and Android phones difficult is that, because many of these phones started out as personal devices, users tend to think, "I paid a lot of money for this, and I'm not going to let you tell me how to use it!" To counter that, many companies nowadays are buying iPhones and Android phones for their users, thinking, "Since it's a corporate phone, we can lock it down however we want." While MDM means that they can lock it down however they want, it doesn't change the fact that the user is still going to expect to be able to do all the awesome, powerful, and fun stuff (and the personal things, too), regardless of who bought the phone.

Furthermore, thanks to the consumerization of IT (and the concept of FUIT), we have to deal with the fact that users are more adept at going rogue and figuring things out on their own. If we don't find a way to accommodate work and personal apps and data on the same device, they will.

We can see that a new issue is emerging: how to satisfy the needs of both users and IT. Clearly, device-level management technology by itself can't always solve this issue. Fortunately, this is what we're going to address in the rest of this book, but first there are several more issues (for both end users and IT) that we need to cover.

Privacy issues

Aside from all the usability problems, many users have issues with how "Big Brother" MDM feels to them. Some of these fears are completely legitimate and are at the heart of the way MDM operates. Other fears are rather absurd and downright overblown (but try explaining that to some users)!

Real privacy issues

One of the big privacy issues that users worry about is MDM tracking their location. It's pretty easy to do, and most MDM solutions can show maps with breadcrumb trails of locations. (Remember that iOS needs an agent app to collect location data, but it's still possible.) Of course, users can always choose to turn off their phone's location services, but many don't know that. (And sometimes MDM policies are created that require location services to be enabled.)

Another real privacy issue is that MDM can see the names of all the apps that are installed on a user's device, as MDM policies might need to do this to carry out app blacklisting or make sure that required corporate apps are install. Users might fear that their companies are able to use that to see the, um, "non-work" apps that they might have installed on their phone—a valid concern to be sure. In this case, there's no way users can prevent this except by un-enrolling their devices or removing personal apps that they don't want their company to know about.

By the way, many jurisdictions have legal protections for employees against employers snooping into their personal lives, which could include collecting location data and personal applications from non-company devices. But this doesn't mean these MDM products can't do this stuff, and users rightly should at least be aware of it.

Imagined privacy issues

One of the most interesting things I came across when writing this book was talking to my non-tech friends about all the things they think their companies can do with their phones. For example, many people believe that IT can read personal emails, text messages, full call logs, or view photos taken with the phone's camera. While some of these things might be possible in certain situations and with certain applications, in reality, this doesn't come up with any of the mainstream MDM vendors.

Remember that with iOS configuration profiles, you can see exactly what is and isn't accessible by an MDM server just by looking at them. So you can easily see that it's impossible to read any email messages, contacts, call logs, or text messages, or to view photos. Sure, some of those things will be accessible in a device backup made with Apple Configurator or iTunes, but since a device has to be unlocked and plugged in via USB to do that, it's a lot harder for a user to unwittingly allow this to happen. Still, explaining this to users can be difficult, especially if they don't trust IT anyway.

Now when it comes to MDM agent apps (either as an optional agent app for iOS or as the core MDM app for Android), things aren't quite so well defined. There are all sorts of things that apps can do. One way to find out what an app can do is to look at the permissions it requests. Remember that in iOS, the app will have to explicitly ask to access location data, contacts, calendars, reminders, and photos, and a user can revoke those permissions at any time. Android apps will list out a lot more permissions, but users don't have granular control, meaning that there's a "take it or leave it" element when accepting the app.

As long as I'm on the topic of unfounded fears, it's worth noting that while many of the things that aren't possible with MDM are, in fact, quite possible using other techniques. For example, MDM software might not be able to read email on a phone, but the IT department can certainly read a user's email directly from the Exchange server. Or consider that while most MDM software itself can't send harvest call logs, most corporate cell phone plans provide a way for the company to get this information directly from the mobile phone company. So some of these far-out user fears of MDM are actually perfectly valid fears of IT.

The reality of privacy issues

In practice, privacy issues like tracking location and viewing user-installed apps will depend on how MDM is implemented by MDM vendors and by IT. Most vendors build controls in their products that are designed to protect user privacy. This might mean that sensitive data is not collected at all, or if data is needed for policies, the policies are executed without actually showing the private data to administrators. There can also be different policies for shared corporate devices that are supposed to stay on-premises versus users' primary devices that they take everywhere they go.

Ultimately, privacy issues will depend on the quality of the relationship between users and their company. Some users may never be convinced, but assuming their company isn't doing faux BYOD (where users *have* to pay for their work phones—a real drag), they're always free to not use their personal phones for work.

The Reality of MDM for IT

The previous section was all about the reality of MDM from the users' perspective. Now I'm going to look at the reality of MDM from your perspective as an IT pro. While IT certainly faces its own set of challenges and complexities around MDM, the good news is that they're not insurmountable. (And truth be told, for the most part, managing the mechanics of mobile devices isn't as difficult as, say, VDI or anything that has to do with Windows.)

The general theme for IT is that there are many more moving parts in enterprise mobility today as opposed to a few years ago, and because of that, there are more places where management isn't as tight as it used to be. There's actually a whole laundry list of items IT has to think about, including:

- MDM for iOS and Android still can't do a lot of things that BlackBerry can do.
- Android fragmentation.
- Rooted and jailbroken devices are tricky.
- It's hard to know which apps are dangerous.

Let's look at these one by one.

MDM is a long way from BlackBerry

MDM for iOS has improved considerably over the past six years, and today it's good enough to cover a wide variety of situations. And despite some unevenness and fragmentation, Android MDM is coming along, too. However, the reality is that both of these are a long way from the degree of manageability available in Black-Berry.

If you're used to all the controls in BlackBerry Enterprise Server, you'll be disappointed with iOS and Android MDM. With BlackBerry, there was never any debate about how "committed to the enterprise" it was. Blackberry also had a huge advantage in that the complete stack—hardware, OS, management protocol, management server—were all vertically integrated. When new features came out, there was always a way for IT to make sure they were used safely.

What are some of the things that BlackBerry can do that are missing in iOS and most versions of Android? For one, on Black-berry, you can actually legitimately blacklist individual apps or group apps instead of using the roundabout method mentioned from Chapter 4. You can prevent apps from accessing location data or other sensitive data, and you can have better controls over telephony and messaging—the list goes on and on. There are even things that you might not think of immediately but that can be important for high-security environments. For example, with BlackBerry, you can make it so that users aren't allowed to have lock-screen notifications that show the contents of emails, or you can make it so that any time the microphone is in use, the red status light will flash. None of this is available with iOS or typical Android MDM today.

Android fragmentation

While Android management has improved in general, fragmentation can still be a difficult issue. Since I already talked about the causes in the last chapter, there's not too much left to add here. Even after taking these fragmentation issues into account, on top of this, you have to deal with the fact that the amount of control possible with an "average" Android device is less than what's possible for iOS.

On a slightly unrelated note, we can also blame fragmentation for the fact that many apps come out on iOS before Android. While there may be more Android devices in the world, fragmentation means that the Apple App Store is a larger single market for developers, and so that's where the effort goes first. This can translate into more problems when you're supporting Android users.

Rooted and jailbroken devices

One of the toughest things for MDM to deal with is jailbroken and rooted devices. There are just too many unknowns: It's not too particularly difficult for users to do, it's not always easy to detect, and if it happens and you're not aware of it, all bets are off when it comes to your management policies.

There are all sorts of reasons why people might want to jailbreak or root their phones, with the most common reason being to get around carrier or device OEM restrictions. Carriers usually either charge a premium or don't even allow customers to tether other devices to a phone's data connection, but this is easily bypassed on jailbroken and rooted devices. iPhone users often want to get around the locked-down Apple world to take advantage of more features or install apps from alternative marketplaces like Cydia. And while most Android devices already allow users to install apps from non-app store locations, many users still root their devices to update to the latest version of Android, which their manufacturer might not support, or to remove carrier "crapware."

While Apple and Google continually try to improve the security of their devices, in the grand scheme of things, rooting and jailbreaking aren't all that difficult for end users to do, and when it happens, who knows what could happen to the corporate data on your phones? Needless to say, these devices are a risk you need to know about.

Many enterprise mobility management products attempt to detect jailbroken devices. They typically do this by looking for certain applications or files or altered settings that wouldn't be on a normal device, or they try to do things that wouldn't normally be possible. However, this detection isn't foolproof, as there's always a back-and-forth "arms race" between the people who root and jailbreak devices and the people who try to detect and stop it.

Because of this, there will be some compromised devices that you won't be able to detect. There are even apps in the underground app stores that specifically exist to lie to MDM software, thus tricking the software into thinking the phone is configured one way when it's actually configured another way.

So how do we deal with this? Some users will be jailbreaking their phones to get cool features, and while this is dangerous, this is less of a concern than people who are jailbreaking their devices to specifically get around management policies. For this second group of people, a re-examination of how we provide access to corporate data might be in order—just like we've been talking about all along in the discussion about users, consumerization, and FUIT.

Finally, there could be a subset of users who purposefully jailbreak their devices with malicious intent towards the company. This is the most difficult to deal with, though really, this isn't an MDM issue but rather a continuing security issue that's been around forever and will continue to exist long into the future.

It's hard to know which apps are dangerous

As much as users hate having IT take away any of their apps, blacklisting isn't always easy for IT, either. First of all, as we discussed in Chapter 4, iOS and Android MDM don't really have a direct and simple way of dealing with user-installed apps. The bigger issue, though, is how do you even know which apps to blacklist?

Of course, you'll want to blacklist apps that are outright malware. And like we've been doing for years, we can admonish users not to click on unknown links or install apps from sketchy third-party app stores and stick to the reasonable safety of Google Play or the Apple App Store. (But it goes without saying that just because an app is in those stores that doesn't mean it's not malware.)

There are app reputation services like Appthority that take into account many different aspects of apps in order to rate them and give more information to help IT make decisions. For example, Appthority looks at how apps behave when running, whether they leave sensitive data unprotected in storage or transmission, what servers apps contact, who built them, app store ratings, and even things like the apps' terms of service. While Appthority can be used as a standalone service, it's also been incorporated into a number of other EMM vendors' products.

Blacklisting and tools like Appthority can help you avoid specific threats, but what about more "normal" apps? Remember that when you have corporate email synced to a device, any other app can access the corporate contacts and calendar, and users can easily share links and attachments with other apps. So are you supposed to blacklist any app that can access these resources or share data in any way? (Because that's most of them, including a lot of your users' favorite apps. One person's malware is another person's killer app!) No amount of selective blacklisting is going to remove this threat. Again, this is a place where an older style of management just won't work in the era of the consumerization of IT.

Where MDM Works Well

After reading the first half of this chapter, you might might be turned off by MDM and think that I hate it. But remember, I love MDM, and so should you! My point is that if you look at what your users are doing with iPhones, iPads, and Android devices and then decide the answer is to use MDM to magically transform them into locked-down corporate devices, that's going to fail big time. (Again, you can be forgiven for thinking this way, since it worked for so long in the past. But in today's world, this just isn't how users work anymore.)

Having said all that, there are many different situations where MDM is the right tool for what needs to be accomplished, and plenty of companies that are happy with what MDM gives them. Some of these scenarios are:

- Provisioning corporate settings, credentials, and apps.
- Kiosks and shared devices.
- Complying with legal requirements.

Provisioning corporate settings, credentials, and apps

MDM is undeniably great for turning iOS and Android devices into corporate-ready devices. Clearly, if you want to use an iPhone or Android device for work, you need to provision corporate settings, and MDM is a great way to do this. We can come up with a whole list of MDM features that help out users.

First, there are the basic security features (which, frankly, users should have anyway), like a pin-code lock and encryption. MDM can guide users into these good practices.

Second, setting up all of the credentials (email accounts, Wi-Fi, VPN, web shortcuts, installing corporate apps, etc.) that are necessary to get a device plugged into the company can be a huge pain for users, especially the less technically savvy ones. MDM takes care of all of this. Then, once all of these credentials have been provisioned, IT can centrally modify them as needed. And of course, when employees leave, MDM can easily remove all the settings and passwords that were configured on a device.

The key to both of these is that the management that comes with MDM is a net gain for the user. Sure, there's a tradeoff involved, like the user has to have a reasonable (not too long) password on the device to get corporate email via the built-in mail app. But overall, the value of that email access and the convenience of getting everything else set up at once far outweighs the pain of having to have that password. There's a big difference between the MDM use described here versus using MDM to "lock down" a device like it was 2003.

Kiosks and shared devices

Most of what I've talked about in terms of MDM so far has concerned users' primary devices—the devices (whether BYOD or corporate) that get used for both work and personal tasks and are carried by users everywhere they go, all the time. Obviously there's a whole class of other use cases that doesn't require the same level of device personalization. These are any devices that aren't expected to be used for personal tasks by a single user, including kiosks, shared devices, and devices that don't go home with anybody at night.

In these cases, MDM isn't just convenient—it's probably a necessity. You'll want to do things to these devices that you wouldn't do to a primary device, like preventing users from installing apps and enabling location tracking to keep users from taking them. This is also where tools like the Apple Configurator or specialized versions of Android can be used.

Complying with legal requirements

Everyone knows that public companies and organizations in industries that deal with sensitive personal and financial information have to deal with complex regulations for security and auditability. Anyone involved in the IT departments of these types of companies also knows that the IT policies that address compliance with legal requirements and the IT policies that actually ensure security are two completely different sets of policies. And, as if that's not challenging enough, most of these legal regulations and laws were written well before iPhones and Android.

So, because compliance and enterprise mobility management are really two different subjects, there are a lot of people who look at MDM simply as a way to be compliant, and in many of those cases, they don't really care about all the "new" ways that users work.

Of course one of the tricky things about complying with all of these various regulations is that every organization interprets the rules a bit differently. Some might decide flat out that no user data can be on a phone with corporate data, regardless of how secure the containers are. (In those cases, old-school locked-down MDM is great. They don't care if users bring in separate personal devices.) Other organizations might decide to just put basic security checks in place and implement a business policy that says that "users should not do anything that can compromise data security." (Whatever that means.) Again, it really depends.

One of the cool things about many regulations (like SOX, HIPAA, or FIPS in the U.S.) is that many of them specifically require things like passwords, password complexity, keeping records about devices, and encryption. And hey, it just so happens that basic MDM offers all of these things! Most of them are right there in iOS's configuration profiles, Android's Device Administration API, and even Exchange ActiveSync.

Of course many regulations also include things that aren't part of devices' MDM APIs—like auditing and keeping records of actions—but nearly all MDM servers add auditing, logging, and reporting capabilities. As a result, nearly all MDM providers claim to be useful for all sorts of regulated industries.

So while these features won't guard your device against many of the real threats, they do serve the legitimate purpose of putting a "yes" in the compliance check box, even if the reasons and requirements are outdated and out of touch.

The Next Step Beyond MDM: Dual Persona

Hopefully by now you can see that while MDM is a good tool for a lot of tasks and different situations, there are some problems it can't solve. The most important of these problems is dealing with personal and corporate data and apps living together on the same device.

The main reason MDM can't solve this is because MDM sets the boundary of management policies at the device level, meaning personal apps are subjected to all the same restrictions as corporate apps (and all of the corporate apps are subject to the same level of control as personal apps). There's just no granularity here.

More important, MDM doesn't provide any way to keep apps from sharing (or leaking!) data with other apps that are on a device. The only way to do this is to just lock it down, and then it's not really solving the problem—it's just ignoring it.

What has emerged is the need to manage and control corporate apps and data separately from personal apps and data. There are many different terms various people use to describe this need—the term that I like to use is "dual persona."

What are the basic requirements for supporting dual persona? Here are the things that you need to be able to do or aspire to:

- Keep tight management over corporate data and applications.
- Give users a choice of devices.
- Support personal devices to the same degree as corporate devices.
- Allow a free and open experience for personal applications.
- Allow flexible deployment models to suit different user preferences.

The rest of the book from here on out is going to cover techniques and ideas about how to enable dual persona on the mobile devices you have to manage.

6. Early Attempts at "Solving" Mobility and Providing Dual Persona

So far in this book, we've identified the need to deliver enterprise applications and data to mobile devices in a way that enables us to control and limit their interaction with personal apps and data. That's what I've decided to call "dual persona," since users have their personal and work "personas" side by side on the same device.

Before we get into what I believe is the "better" way to handle dual persona, I want to look at some of the less-than-ideal ways in which the industry has tried to achieve this goal in the past. In this chapter, we'll examine three such attempts: remote Windows desktop applications, web apps, and virtualized OSes on mobile devices.

Delivering Windows Apps and Desktops to Mobile Devices via Remote Computing

One of the earliest attempts to get work apps onto personal phones and tablets was to use the tried-and-true corporate technology known as remoting (or remote desktops). In this case, the mobile device connects to some server or remote host (or even the user's own desktop PC) that sends the screen images of the Microsoft Windows environment down to the phone, and all of the user's key presses and gestures are sent up to the remote host. To someone who doesn't know how this works, it looks like "Hey! I'm running Windows on my iPad." But really the user is just connecting to a remote copy of Windows running somewhere else.

There are a lot of different products that can provide this type of remote Windows technology. Also called desktop virtualization or VDI technology, you can provide remote desktops with products like Citrix XenDesktop, VMware Horizon View, Dell vWorkspace, or Microsoft Remote Desktop. Or you might have heard of the protocols that actually handle the remoting, including RDP, ICA, HDX, PCoIP, and VNC. Or you might know one of the many consumer-oriented products that offer this kind of functionality, like Citrix GoToMyPC, LogMeIn, and pcAnywhere.

Considering that companies like Citrix and VMware had this technology entrenched in the enterprise when iPhones, iPads, and Android devices first came out, it's easy to see why delivering remote Windows applications to mobile phones was the first proposed solution. It's like the whole desktop virtualization industry joined in unison to say, "Hey, we got this! You can use remote desktop. Problem solved." And while remoting Windows does indeed solve many of the problems of getting corporate applications to mobile devices, the process of doing that unfortunately creates many more problems.

Advantages of accessing remote Windows apps on mobile devices

At first glance, accessing a remote Windows application or Windows desktop seems to solve most of the dual persona problems. Since no corporate information lives on the device, there's no need to lock down the user experience or even to manage the device at all. There's no need to figure out how to control data moving around inside the mobile device, since it's all contained within the remote Windows desktop. Admins can enable policies on the server or on the remote desktop connection broker to disable client-side clipboard mapping, USB port mapping, and drive mapping. The overall idea is that you can deliver any Windows desktop application you already have to any device, without having to be concerned about the device's capabilities (since remote desktop clients exist for every type of device imaginable) or without making any changes to your existing desktop applications.

Disadvantages of accessing remote Windows apps on mobile devices

While delivering remote Windows desktops to phones and tablets seems like a decent and easy way to provide a dual persona environment, in the real world, it's actually not that great.

First of all, using remote Windows apps and desktops obviously requires a network connection. And while some people love to talk about how ubiquitous connectivity is right around the corner, I just don't buy it. There are just too many times I can't get a connection, such as when I'm riding the subway, on a plane, or in a random room that doesn't have great Wi-Fi or 3G/4G coverage. Without an Internet connection, remote Windows apps don't work.

Second, and more important, Windows desktop applications were designed for devices with large screens, keyboards, and precision pointing devices (like mice or trackpads). Sure, users can use the virtual keyboard on their phones or tablets, but doing so covers up half of their already highly valuable screen real estate on the mobile devices. And sure, some people like to carry around

Bluetooth keyboards and those little origami cases and stands that they fold together, but then they have to deal with batteries and Bluetooth pairing and the fact that these screen contraptions are always falling apart. And let's face it, if you have to carry around all that stuff to make your iPad act more like a laptop, why not just buy an Ultrabook with a real keyboard?

Even if you get the keyboard part figured out, remember that Windows desktops and applications are designed to be used with a precision pointing device with pixel-level precision—not a human finger. If you try to use your finger as a pointing device for Windows, you often have to peck around while trying to hit the right button. (Unless you just zoom way in, but then you spend half your time just zooming and panning around the desktop.)

The other thing to keep in mind is that when it comes to the mobile apps that users use on a daily basis—email, browsers, and document editing and sharing—users already have really awesome native applications for iOS and Android. Those native apps work offline, and they have great touch-based interfaces with just the right amount of functionality. This makes it hard to deploy a remote Windows app as your corporate "solution" with a straight face, since a user can go to the app store and find dozens of apps that do all the exact same things but that are made for little mobile devices. (Not to mention that these native apps take advantage of all the computing power that's available locally. Gone are the days when phones were too weak to do any "real" work.)

Oh yeah, and desktop virtualization is a complex technology

The final downside to using remote Windows as your solution for corporate apps on mobile devices is that the technology is complex. I was a co-author of an entire book about Windows desktop virtualization. (Called *The VDI Delusion*, it came out in 2012. Look it up!) Needless to say, desktop virtualization is some pretty elaborate stuff, with many different products and lots of engineering required to get everything working. It's not too practical to go through all of the pain and expense of desktop virtualization just to enable a few Windows apps on some iPhones. Doing so is like killing an ant with a sledgehammer—effective, but overkill.

Legacy applications: Where remote Windows desktops shine

Despite all of the difficulties and downfalls of delivering remote Windows desktop applications to phones and tablets, there are actually some scenarios where this technology makes sense and that are worth mentioning here so you don't think that I completely hate Windows.

While it's unreasonable to expect users to accept remote keyboard-and-mouse-based Windows desktop applications for their day-to-day tasks like email, there are still plenty of corporate applications that are only available in the form of Windows desktop versions. And let's face it, if those apps are only available as Windows desktop applications in 2013, there's probably a really good reason for it. (If it were possible to convert that app to an iOS, Android, or web app, it probably would have been done by now.) So you can almost say that, by definition, if you need a certain Windows desktop application today, you're probably going to need that Windows application for a long time.

The real question for these important Windows desktop applications is how important is it that your users have access to them from mobile devices? And how good does that user experience have to be? If the desktop application was developed in an era in which users used it only from their desks, can't they continue to use it from their desks? (Meaning you don't have to figure out how to make it work from a phone.)

And if you need to provide mobile access to a Windows desktop application only for very occasional or emergency use, maybe this desktop virtualization technology is fine and users can just live with the inconvenience. After all, if they're out in the park with their kids and they need to do something with a Windows desktop application, struggling to use the tiny phone screen is not as inconvenient as going home to get their laptop.

The bottom line is that there are some good, solid reasons to consider delivering remote Windows desktop applications to users' phones and tablets—it's just that those reasons are for very specific use cases, not blanket ways to "solve" the dual persona challenge on all mobile devices.

Transforming Windows desktop apps for mobile use

While we're on the topic of remote Windows applications, there's one final thing worth mentioning. For those (hopefully few) cases where you absolutely must provide a remote Windows desktop application to a user who will access it via a phone or tablet, there are some technology add-ons to these desktop virtualization and remote Windows products that can help make the Windows keyboard-and-mouse-based desktop applications a bit easier to use on mobile touch-based devices.

The first example would be adaptations made by remote Windows desktop client apps for iOS and Android themselves. Citrix, VMware, and others try to add features to their mobile client apps that make using remote Windows desktop applications more pleasant for mobile users. For example, they might "scrape" the contents of the remote Windows Start Menu and populate a local app menu on the mobile client so users can launch apps in a familiar way instead of having to navigate a remote Start Menu via a tiny screen and their fat finger. Or these clients might invoke the mobile device's local drop-down list selector wheel instead of rendering the remote one whenever the remote application's drop-down box functionality is chosen.

There are also dedicated products in the market that have become broadly known as "app refactoring" tools, which can help transform the user interface of the remote Windows application to make it more touch- and mobile-friendly. These tools work in concert with your VDI or remote Windows environment to do things like making the buttons of applications bigger (and easier to use with your fingers). They can also rearrange and hide buttons that aren't used as much, again generally making the application's layout as touch-friendly as possible.

Some examples of app refactoring tools are the Citrix XenApp Mobility Pack and Framehawk's application mobilization platform. The XenApp Mobility Pack can be used to configure Windows desktop application interfaces, which are delivered via Citrix's standard remote protocol environments. Framehawk goes a step further by using a proprietary protocol that was built from the ground up to support mobile app interfaces. Other people have used the app customization features of AppSense's DesktopNow, applications' built-in menus or ribbon customizations, or even Windows' own built-in Accessibility tools to customize UI elements to make them easier to use without physical keyboards and mice.

Make no mistake: Delivering individual Windows desktop applications or entire Windows desktops to a phone or tablet is an awesome party trick. And if you need immediate mobile access to a specific application, it can be an instant win. But as a serious long-term solution to accommodating dual persona and solving mobility, it just doesn't cut it and should be limited to the few applications that absolutely must run on the Microsoft Windows platform.

Web Apps and HTML5

Another way that many enterprises attempt to extend their existing applications to mobile devices is via the web, as delivering web apps to mobile devices is often perceived as an "easy" way to separate work apps from personal stuff on the devices.

When it comes to actually delivering web apps to mobile devices, a lot of people get excited about HTML5. While it's true that HTML5 technology can enable some amazing device-independent web apps, keep in mind that most web apps in today's corporate environments are *not* HTML5—they're just regular old-fashioned websites and web apps. (Think about your web email system, your expense reporting system, your intranet, etc.)

The double-edged sword with regular (non-HTML5) web apps is that, since they're already in place today, it's easy for companies to say, "Oh, fantastic! We don't actually need to do anything special to deliver these apps to mobile devices because all the mobile devices already have browsers. So we're all set!"

Of course this is the exact same trap you fall into when you try to "solve" your mobile access to Windows desktop applications by just delivering the existing Windows apps to mobile devices. Sure, your corporate web apps might technically "work" from mobile devices (assuming there aren't any issues with browser requirements or plugins), and it might be possible to get the mobile devices onto the VPN or to deliver a secure browser to them, but how usable are these web apps from mobile devices really? Needless to say, it depends on the specific app.

So while just using your existing web apps might seem like a solution to your "mobility problem," it could also be a horrible experience that causes users to go out and find their own applications. So whether it actually solves anything in your environment remains to be seen.

What about HTML5?

Whenever people talk about the future of web apps or the new or cool types of web apps, HTML5-based apps come up. There are a lot of reasons to be excited—HTML5 can solve a lot of the issues that traditional web apps have on mobile devices.

First, while many old-style websites might not work well (or even work at all) for a mobile device, HTML5 has features that make it easier to adapt. There are APIs for dealing with touch events, screen orientation, and geolocation, and the canvas element makes it easier to draw "mobile"-looking interfaces.

And while traditional web apps don't work offline, modern HTML5-based web apps can. In fact, this whole book was written in an HTML5 app—Google Docs—and much of the work was done offline. (I'm writing this sentence via the Chrome web browser, offline, from flight level 350 somewhere between San Francisco and Toronto.)

HTML5 is also a widely implemented standard—a standard that has done away with many browser plugins—meaning we can finally say that these apps will run anywhere, on any device.

And since HTML5 apps are web apps, they are logistically easy to develop. You don't have to deal with the complexities of building a desktop virtualization environment, and you don't need to deal with all the restrictions of native application distribution and vendor app stores that we talked about back in Chapter 3.

The reality of HTML5 for enterprise mobile apps

After reading this, you might be excited and think that HTML5 would be the perfect way to deliver all your enterprise apps to your mobile devices. After all, HTML5 can help separate work data from personal data, it's well suited for mobile, and it's platform-independent. The same app will work for iOS and Android and whatever else comes along in a few years—a huge selling point!

Naturally, there are a few caveats. Sure, compared with traditional web apps (and remote Windows desktops, like we talked about before), HTML5 apps may be pretty awesome. But you have to keep in mind that users will really be comparing them to native iOS and Android apps, and today the functionality of HTML5 apps are a few years behind what's possible with native mobile apps.

However, do our "work" apps really need all of the latest whiz-bang features that native local apps can provide? The answer varies depending on the app. There's a broad swath of enterprise apps that would be great as HTML5 apps, especially in situations where it may not be worthwhile to write native iOS and Android apps but where creating one HTML5 app would be a huge improvement over the alternatives of old-style web apps, remote Windows apps, or having no mobile access at all.

On the other hand, for certain critical everyday apps, HTML5 won't cut it—there are just too many other challenges. Take email, for example. The Outlook Web App has gotten a whole lot better recently, and Exchange 2013's version works great on mobile devices. But while it works offline on some desktop browsers, it doesn't work offline with any mobile browsers yet. The Gmail HTML5 app has offline support for some browsers, but not others.

Another problem is that even though these HTML5 apps work offline, if you want the latest mail messages to be available offline, you need to have the browser open before you go offline. The same is true on the flip side—if you compose or reply to any new messages while offline, you need to have your browser open when you reconnect for the messages to be sent. This also means that these HTML5 email apps can't get push notifications.

Also, while HTML5 browsers are ubiquitous, not all browsers support all features. To be clear, compatibility is much better than it used to be, and not having to deal with as many plugins as before is great, but there are still some issues. One of the biggest ones is around offline storage. Not all HTML5 apps that are supposed to work offline will work with all browsers. And if you're not managing the browser, it can be difficult to control how HTML5 interacts with the rest of the device, and securing local storage can be problematic.

Overall, HTML5 can be great for many apps, just not super-important ones like email.

HTML5 in managed browsers and hybrid apps

All the talk about HTML5 apps so far has assumed that users are just accessing them from whatever unmanaged browser they happen to have on their mobile devices. But it's actually possible to do a lot more if you can control the browser "shell" in which the HTML5 app runs. This can be done using a managed corporate browser app (which I'll cover in Chapter 8) or through hybrid apps that combine HTML5 code with native apps. Hybrid apps can give HTML5 apps access to push notifications and other native features, and can be managed and distributed like native apps.

Mobile Virtualization

The final way that folks have tried to create a dual persona environment on mobile devices is mobile virtualization, an umbrella term for a set of technologies that allows IT and users to each have their own complete separate environments to manage and use as they see fit. This is conceptually similar to the days when users carried two phones—one work and one personal—only now those two phones are virtual and run side by side on a single piece of hardware.

There are several different vendors offering mobile virtualization products, and they all work a bit differently. Some have two complete virtual instances of an operating system running side by side; some use one operating system running on top of another; and some use a common kernel and only virtualize the user space. Needless to say, this level of modification is not anything that Apple will ever allow to happen to iOS, so mobile virtualization is limited to devices that run Android.

If you're like me, your first thought on hearing about mobile virtualization is, "There's no way a phone would ever have enough power to do this!" But there are a few reasons why mobile virtualization isn't quite as resource-heavy as it might seem. First, the obvious one: Phones are pretty powerful these days. While virtualization was a stretch just a few years ago, today's devices have plenty of horsepower to spare. More important, even though mobile virtualization means that a single device has multiple OS instances or profiles, the multitasking scheme is usually the same as with a device running a single version of Android in the traditional way. There's still only one foreground app running at any time, so the device doesn't actually have to do that much more work. Also, in the case of "lighter" solutions that virtualize only the user space, much of the OS is shared between the virtual environments anyway.

Regardless of which mobile virtualization technique is used, the result is that there are completely separate work and personal environments on the same Android phone. IT can lock down the "work side" as much as it wants using all the MDM tools and techniques discussed in Chapter 4, and this is okay because the users have the "other side" as their personal space where they can do whatever they want. With mobile virtualization, IT usually takes care of provisioning the work environment itself and sets policies for how the two environments interact with each other. Often, contacts and notifications are shared, and some solutions allow work app shortcuts to appear in the personal environment.

Because the device keeps the two environments completely separated, there's no need to worry about using remote Windows apps or web apps to try to keep corporate and personal data separated—you can just use whatever mobile apps you would use on a normal device. This is one of the biggest selling points of mobile virtualization.

The reality of mobile virtualization

So this mobile virtualization concept sounds pretty great, right? Unfortunately, there are some pretty significant drawbacks. First, as mentioned before, is the fact that these solutions are Android-only right now. This means that if you adopt mobile virtualization, your solution is only going to work for half of your users. Then you'll have to figure out some other way to deal with the iOS devices. And if you figure out "some other way" that's acceptable to you, why wouldn't you just use that other way for both iOS and Android to have one solution for both?

Another issue is that all of these mobile virtualization solutions require heavily modified versions of Android. To get the modified OS on a device without rooting it, the mobile virtualization vendors have to partner with device manufacturers. This means that dual persona virtualization will be limited to a few specific devices from specific manufacturers. So for it to work, all of your users have to have these particular devices. This flies against the idea of BYOD, consumerization, and end-user choice, and it's the No. 1 reason why dual persona virtualization will never be widespread.

The final issue with mobile virtualization is that there's no granularity within the work environment. In other words, you're going to have some of the same problems that you'd have when you use device-level MDM on non-virtualized devices. For example, if one app needs to have a very high level of security, it would force the entire environment to live under that high level of security. So that 16-character password that protects sensitive financial data? Users would have to use that if they want to do a quick glance at their work inbox, too. (Though one mobile virtualization vendor, Cellrox, addresses this issue by setting up multiple work personas that can each have management policies.)

Mobile virtualization for corporate devices?

All is not lost with mobile virtualization, though. If you don't have to worry about accommodating BYOD or device choice, mobile virtualization could absolutely be a better alternative than locking down non-virtualized mobile devices. Think about it from the users' perspective. If they had a choice between a totally locked down corporate device or a totally locked down corporate device with a side personal area where they can do whatever they want, most would choose the latter.

Mobile virtualization alternatives

In addition to the mobile virtualization products based on highly modified versions of Android, there are a few other products in the market that use different techniques to provide similar functionality. For example, Samsung has a modified version of Android called KNOX that provides work and personal separation, but only apps that are signed by Samsung are allowed to run in the corporate environment. BlackBerry 10 also has built-in capabilities for dual persona side-by-side work and personal environments. (The vendor has been doing some version of this for a couple of years now, which is pretty awesome!) Unfortunately, BlackBerry 10 is at a disadvantage because of its tiny market share and small number of third-party apps. Like mobile virtualization, these solutions don't help if you're trying to deal with BYOD or allow users a choice of devices, but they're still a "nicer" alternative to traditional company-provided locked-down devices.

Conclusion: There Must Be Another Way

Remote Windows desktop applications, traditional web apps, HTML5 apps, and mobile virtualization all legitimately address the need to enable dual persona on mobile devices, and there are places where each of these three technologies works quite well. But when it comes to mainstream solutions, we still need to keep looking for a way to separate work and personal environments— with a native experience—on any device. That brings us to our next topic, something called mobile app management.

7. Mobile App Management

We established back in Chapter 5 that our ultimate goal is to manage corporate apps and data independently from personal apps and data on our users' mobile devices. In the last chapter, I looked at some of the methods for doing that: desktop virtualization, web apps, and mobile virtualization. Unfortunately, each one of those options has its flaws. In this chapter, I'll look at another method of managing corporate resources separately from personal resources: the technology known as mobile app management (or MAM).

Like the techniques outlined in the previous chapters, MAM gets you a step closer to managing what you care about and not having to manage what you don't care about. (This is a good thing!) MAM brings the perimeter closer to the corporate resources, rather than casting a wide net around the whole device.

App Stores and MDM as MAM

One of the initial ways that people think about managing apps is centered on controlling who is actually allowed to access and install certain apps. One way to control access is by creating an app store. An app store isn't anything fancy—really it's nothing more than a list of links to wherever apps happen to be hosted. The list itself can contain mobile apps, web apps, or just a set of pages on your corporate intranet.

Obviously, if you're distributing any in-house or custom apps that aren't available in public app stores, you'll want to have some sort of mechanism to allow users to download and find those apps. This is where an app store comes into play.

App stores often have some sort of mechanism that authenticates users so they can get access to different apps depending on their identity. This is essential for any app signed with an iOS Developer Enterprise Certificate, as Apple requires that those apps are used only by employees of the company that signed them. If you're using Apple's Volume Purchase Program or B2B apps, an app store can be used to ensure that the right people get access to the redemption links or codes.

App stores can also be useful for linking to any free public apps that users in your company might need to do their jobs—for example, front-end clients for SaaS or other enterprise apps your company has.

While app stores can manage apps by controlling who has access to them, one of the problems with them is that once users install these apps, there's nothing an app store can do to uninstall the apps. So all the role-based access stuff is great, but once an app is out there, how are you going to remove it from the device when the time comes?

Of course, MDM happens to provide a few ways to do this. Remember from Chapter 4 that if you're managing an iOS device, you can use that MDM connection to prompt the device to install or remove apps. (Apple unsurprisingly calls these "managed apps.") In this case, a user would select an app in the corporate app store, the app store would tell the MDM server to install the app as a "managed app," and it could subsequently be removed by the MDM server or when the device is removed from management.

Unfortunately, this works only for iOS devices that are managed over the air using full MDM connections. If a user installs an app on an unmanaged device, or if the app store isn't integrated with an MDM server, there's no way for you to remotely uninstall the app. And remember from earlier in the book that MDM for both iOS and Android usually isn't very good at dealing with user-installed apps in general, so blacklisting the app isn't a reliable technique, either.

So how do you deal with removing apps from devices? This is where real mobile app management comes into play. The answer is that you need to modify the behavior of the actual apps, not just try to control access to them. Instead of having to remove an app via MDM, the app itself can have an authentication mechanism, so you just take away a user's access rights. (So the app itself isn't removed—it's just that the user can't authenticate and use it.) Or the app can have a remote kill switch that disables it after a command is sent.

You can see that using app stores and managing apps with MDM is very different from using "real" MAM to control apps' behavior. The reason why I'm making this distinction is that some people use the term "mobile app management" to refer to both of these techniques, and this can be misleading. Yes, technically app stores and MDM can manage applications, and these are indeed important, but clearly this is very different from the type of MAM that I'll cover in the next section.

You also probably noticed that app stores and MDM don't do anything about the dual persona issue, either. Again, this is where you need to be able to modify app behavior. With that, let's dive into mobile app management.

Mobile App Management Concepts

As we look at managing individual apps, you'll notice that there's a lot to this that sounds very similar to MDM. Mobile app management vendors will talk about passwords and authentication, encryption, VPNs, remote disabling of apps, conditional policies like geofencing, and the ability to do all of these management tasks wirelessly over the air.

The key concept with MAM is that all this is implemented in individual apps, rather than on the device. So now, whether or not the device is managed is less important—what you care most about is that the device has a network connection so you can communicate with the apps. Furthermore, besides just shrinking the perimeter of management down to the app level, app management can go above and beyond the capabilities offered by the device. Instead of being limited to the APIs provided by the OS, you can build anything you want into the app (as long as it still respects the OS's app sandbox). All this means that sensitive apps can be locked down without impairing the user's experience on the rest of the device.

The greatest benefit from this type of MAM is that you get to decide how much and under what circumstances an app shares data, solving the primary dual persona issue. You don't have to worry about users' personal apps leaking data, because the corporate data is contained in managed apps and is inaccessible to unmanaged apps.

Let's run down a laundry list of typical MAM features and look at how they work. Keep in mind that I'm not describing a single MAM product, but rather providing a general overview. Here's what we'll look at:

- App configuration
- Passwords and authentication
- VPN
- Encryption
- Remote app disable
- Conditional policies

• Data sharing

Just like with MDM, many MAM features require some sort of policy server or management console that uses an over-the-air connection to monitor the state of apps, issue commands for management tasks, and configure and execute policies.

App configuration

Some MAM features don't have to be turned on—instead, they're just baked in from the start and already present. For example, while you have to specifically tell a device to require a password, an app can be preconfigured to use a password no matter what. (The last section of this chapter will cover all the techniques for creating manageable apps.)

Passwords and authentication

App-level passwords can provide users with granular access. For example, if there's no password on an unmanaged device, the corporate mail client can still be protected with a password. Or there can be just a four-digit pin for the device but a longer, more complex password for a sensitive financial app. Beyond just plain passcodes, requiring logins for apps can ensure that only authorized users can access corporate resources. Some MAM solutions can also provide single sign-on capabilities between corporate apps.

VPN

Instead of relying on a device-wide VPN, individual apps can make connections to corporate networks through VPNs. This has the added benefit of keeping random personal apps out of the corporate network. When mobile devices are in the office, they can connect to a guest or public network and still take advantage of app-level VPNs. (iOS 7 will have a built-in per-app VPN, but we don't know how it will work at the time of writing.)

Encryption

Most devices today offer encryption, but again, this relies on MDM being in place to ensure the device is password-protected. Just like all the other features we've been going over, having encryption built into the app means that company data is encrypted even if the whole device isn't. A lot of MAM solutions also go further by using encryption that's stronger than what's offered by the device.

Remote app disable

Since most of the time it's not possible to actually make an app remove itself, remotely disabling an app usually means disabling it in some other way. Of course, an app has to be running and online to send a command, so remotely disabling an app is often more a matter of the app not running except when it has received specific authorization within a certain period of time.

Conditional policies

There are all sorts of ways to change the behavior of an app under certain circumstances. One of the most common examples is geofencing, or using location data from the device to change the app. For example, an electronic medical records app could have a policy so that it cannot be opened while off hospital grounds. There are limitless other possibilities for conditional policies: They can take into account whether or not a device is managed, the time of day, or whether a device is online. That information can then be used to determine whether an app is allowed to run, whether it works offline, or whether or not any other features work. The logic to implement these policies can be executed on remote management servers, or it can be built entirely into the app so there's no need for a network connection.

Data sharing

As I established, controlling app-to-app interaction is one of the most important aspects of MAM. Remember from Chapter 3 that some of the ways apps can communicate with each other include device-wide frameworks for things like contacts, copy and paste, photos, and document sharing. If you don't want users' random apps to access corporate data, the answer is simple: Don't let corporate apps put any clear data into these device-wide frameworks.

Instead, corporate apps can communicate directly with each other using various other techniques, effectively creating ad hoc corporate frameworks. Or if a corporate app does use a device-provided framework, it can encrypt the data first, so that only other corporate apps will be able to decrypt it.

The most common examples of MAM data sharing are controlling cut and paste, opening documents, and opening links so they can happen only between corporate apps.

Techniques for Creating Apps That Work With MAM

Now that we've covered all that mobile app management can do, let's look at where these apps come from. Of course, the vast majority (like 99.99%) of all the apps in the Apple App Store or Google Play don't have these features, and we also know that it's impossible to get in between a user's device and the public app stores, so these features can't easily be added to any random app.

So how do we get apps that have all these great MAM features? There are five basic routes:

- Basic apps directly from MAM vendors.
- Use a MAM SDK when building new apps.
- App wrapping to add MAM features to existing apps.
- Apps from ISVs that partner with MAM vendors.
- Apps that already have management features but don't require a MAM solution.

Basic apps directly from MAM vendors

Many MAM vendors provide their own versions of everyday "basic" apps like email clients, browsers, and file-syncing apps. These will usually include all of the basic MAM features discussed previously, but since they're built by the MAM vendor, there are opportunities for deeper integration and cool features. (The next chapter is going to cover these core apps in-depth.)

MAM SDKs

If you're building an in-house app from scratch (or having some-body build it for you), you can build in all the MAM features right from the start. MAM vendors typically offer an SDK or app-prep-aration tool that contains all the necessary elements.

App wrapping

If you'd like to manage an app that has already been built by somebody else, you can use a special tool to "wrap" all of the MAM features around the core of the app. To do this, you need to have access to the unsigned app binary. This means that it's not possible to wrap apps that come from public app stores. To obtain these unsigned, wrappable app binaries, you'll have to go directly to ISVs or app developers and ask to purchase the app directly from them, instead of from public app stores. Are mobile app vendors willing to play along? The answer can vary widely, and we'll spend a lot more time on this subject in Chapter 9. For now, we're just talking about the techniques themselves.

Anyway, assuming you can get your hands on the unsigned app binaries, after the app is wrapped, it gets resigned and distrib-uted as an in-house app. Most app wrapping tools do the basics of encryption, remote kill switches, authentication, or app-level VPNs. However, some tools can go a lot further by intercepting, blocking, or spoofing API calls made by the app to really have control over every aspect of its behavior.

For example, if an app calls for the camera, the wrapper can tell the app that the camera isn't available, or the wrapper can just give the app a default image. Or if a user tries to copy text out of the app, the wrapper can intercept and obfuscate it before it gets to the device's clipboard. There are all sorts of cool things you can do, but as you can imagine, it can all get pretty complex pretty fast, and if you try to get too fancy, you could end up breaking the app. Clearly, in a lot of cases, it's preferable to use apps that were built with the corporate requirements in mind, but when that's not possible, app wrapping is good to have.

Apps from partner ISVs

Another important option is to have MAM vendors partner with ISVs directly. Both parties can work together to make sure that management features are implemented in a good way, and then IT departments don't have to worry about obtaining unsigned apps directly. This is a lot smoother, but it still depends on ISVs being onboard with MAM. The problem is that there are at least a dozen MAM vendors out there, and none of their management hooks are compatible with each other. You do the math. There are some issues, but again, since this chapter is just the "theory of MAM techniques," I'll leave that discussion for Chapter 9.

Apps that don't need to be managed

Finally, it's worth mentioning that a lot of apps out there have management features built in but don't need to be hooked into a mobile app management platform. Client-server apps like Salesforce or the Concur travel and expense app are good examples. These apps are freely available for anyone to download, and this is fine because they don't do anything on their own without a backend service that's controlled by the company. They require users to authenticate, (so you don't have to worry about unauthorized access at the app level), and if someone is fired, you just shut off the account on the back end and suddenly the app is useless. For most of these types of apps, you won't have to worry about wrapping or managing them, since they're fine as is.

Conclusion

By now you can see how mobile app management is superior to the dual persona techniques we discussed in the previous chapter. Remote desktops, web apps, and virtualized mobile devices each have their place in the EMM world, but MAM has distinct advantages in that it works across all versions of Android (and, of course, iOS), and native apps provide a superior user experience.

Of course, there are some issues that MAM has to deal with, too, but ultimately the benefits outweigh those in many cases. We'll dig into this in Chapter 9.

8. The Core Apps for MAM: Email Clients, Mobile File Syncing, and Managed Browsers

So far we've talked about mobile app management in broad terms—everything up to this point could apply to any MAM-compatible app. But the reality is that not all apps are created equal, and some mobile apps are much more important than others.

Three such apps are email and calendar clients, mobile file syncing apps, and managed mobile web browsers. If you're looking at doing app management on mobile devices in your environment, chances are good that you're probably looking at these apps—which makes sense, since these are the three basic tools that most users use on their mobile devices to get a lot of their everyday work done.

Fortunately, since these three types of mobile apps are so critical, most vendors that do MAM offer versions of these apps that are pre-built to work with their management platforms so there's no need to re-develop custom apps or mess around with app wrapping. This means that deploying these three core apps is super-easy.

You know the 80/20 rule, where you can get 80% of a result with 20% of the effort, and getting that last 20% is actually where 80% of the work is? Well, this is like that, but it's probably more like 99/1 instead of 80/20. You can probably get 99% of your secure mobile access to the enterprise solved with 1% of the effort through these three mobile apps.

Since these three apps are so important, this chapter is going to take a detailed look at specific issues that come up for each one.

Mobile Email Clients

Email is particularly interesting because how you decide to approach it will be a big factor in what the rest of your enterprise mobility management strategy will look like. Unfortunately, there are some factors that make securing and managing email (especially on iOS devices) difficult, and so there have to be some compromises somewhere.

Why is email so difficult?

I wrote earlier in general terms about how, despite sandboxing, apps on modern mobile devices have many ways to share data, and this data sharing is difficult or impossible to control with MDM. In the case of email, the built-in default apps in iOS and Android share with the rest of the device contact lists, calendar items, task lists, the ability to send messages, the ability to share attachments, and the ability to cut and paste text. This sharing is facilitated by other built-in apps (like the calendar and contacts apps) and APIs (like the clipboard or document sharing).

This openness and integration between apps makes for a great "sharing" experience for users' personal social media apps, but of course on the flip side, it provides just as many ways to leak corporate data. (One person's definition of "integrated sharing" is another person's definition of "data leakage.") For instance, any random app can access contacts and task lists placed on the device by a corporate Exchange account. (The go-to example is a social media app called Path, which was in the news because it takes a user's address book, copies it to its external cloud service, and spams everyone to sign up.) Users do have to explicitly give apps permission for the apps to access some of these frameworks, but many people are used to just hitting "yes" any time an app asks for any permission.

And remember, there's not much that MDM can do about this. In iOS, configuration profiles can be used to prevent users from using one email account to forward messages from another, and third-party apps can be blocked from using an account to send messages. That's it. Users can prevent individual apps from accessing contacts, calendars, and task lists, but only if they choose to do so on their own—iOS configuration profiles can't touch those settings.

For many companies (especially those bound by compliance regulations), having all that corporate "gold" in built-in email, calendar, and contact apps is truly dangerous. How are you supposed to prevent third-party apps from accessing that data? Your only option would be to lock down the device so that data-leaking third-party apps can't be installed. But of course that's not acceptable to users and comes with its own set of difficulties, not the least of which is that many of the most popular iOS and Android apps have the ability to leak corporate data. So what are you supposed to do?

Enter the third-party email clients

While it's impossible to have enough control over what the device's built-in clients do with email and related data, there is another option: Do not use the built-in mail, contacts, and calendar apps for corporate accounts.

Instead, you can deploy third-party securable, manageable email, contacts, and calendar apps rather than using the leaky built-in ones. (Let users use the built-in capabilities for their personal stuff that you don't care about.) This concept is often called a "sandboxed" email client because the email client (and its related

PIM friends) keeps its data locked up inside itself and does not share it with other apps. Most of these MAM products that use sandboxed email clients also allow you to control whether users can copy text from the sandboxed environment, how the "open in" functionality works for attachments, and whether any of this is shared with the device's central repository. This is essentially applying all of the MAM concepts discussed in the previous chapter.

Of course, if you put a sandboxed email client in place, you also have to ensure that users can't get around it by simply manually configuring the built-in mail client on their own. So typically you'd also configure your Exchange settings (or your Exchange ActiveSync Client Access Rules) to ensure that only your chosen third-party app is allowed to access mailboxes (i.e., you'd disable IMAP, POP, etc.). Then the third-party client itself can be managed via your vendor's MAM protocol and/or Exchange Active-Sync MDM policies (with the ActiveSync "device" actually being your third-party app on the client device).

Drawbacks to third-party email clients

These third-party email clients solve a lot of security issues, but unfortunately for users, there are some significant drawbacks as well. One of the biggest problems with third-party email apps on iOS is their inability to download messages in the background.

A full push email experience has always been a killer feature for any mobile platform. (The makers of BlackBerry certainly knew this 15 years ago!) There's no waiting for the device to download emails—there's just an alert, and when you pick up your device, all the messages are there, complete and ready to read. This means that even when you don't have a connection (like when you're in a subway tunnel or on an airplane), you can still see all the emails you received up until the time you lost the connection, even if you didn't happen to do one last check right before the connection was dropped.

People have loved this push experience for years. BlackBerry used its own network operations center and protocol to do it.

With Exchange ActiveSync, the built-in email app on iOS can do this, too. (The same goes for Android.)

The problem is with third-party email clients on iOS. Downloading email messages in the background is not currently an approved use of iOS multitasking. So while third-party corporate email apps may be secure, users don't like them because they have to open them and then wait a few seconds for new messages to download before they can read them. Imagine how annoying this is! Sure, it's possible to use the Apple Push Notification Service to get push notifications that contain the sender, subject line, and a few words of the message, but doing this requires jumping through a few hoops and some extra infrastructure, and you still don't get the full message content! (Because these issues are inherent to all third-party iOS email apps, you can see why some MAM companies want to stay out of the email app business, because no matter what, the app is always going to have this problem and look bad, even though it's Apple's fault.)

Fortunately, this will change when iOS 7 is released, because Apple is opening multitasking up to all apps. (This was the feature that I was most excited to learn about from the Apple Worldwide Developers Conference 2013.) Once again, though, we have to remember that the details won't be public for a few more months, and that there could be some other unknown catches.

(All this is in contrast to Android, where third-party email apps have always been permitted to run and download messages in the background. I know several people who switched from iPhones to Android phones just because of this one single feature.)

Background downloads and a full push experience will make third-party email apps on iOS much more acceptable to users, but unfortunately, there are still other issues to consider.

You might think that building an email app is pretty straightforward, but quite frankly, a lot of the third-party email apps are ugly, not user-friendly, or just flat-out missing features. After all, these are made by companies that your users have never heard of while the built-in mail clients are made by Apple and Google.

Of course this doesn't mean it's impossible to make great third-party email apps—look at how much people love apps like Mailbox. Personally, I use the Gmail iOS app, and I really like it. You just have to hope that the makers of the email apps that are compatible with your MAM platform have actually put in some effort. Some third-party iOS email app makers add features that the built-in apps don't have in order to make them more attractive. But again, whether that works for you depends on your MAM vendor and what's important to your users.

Another issue is that some users really like having a universal inbox that combines work and personal accounts, so unless the third-party app has ways of securely combining these two things (and I don't personally know of any that do), some users might dislike having to go to separate apps for each one. And if all the contacts are sealed inside a third-party app, it could make dealing with text messages and calls a little awkward. A lot of users deal with this by adding important work contacts to their personal contact lists anyway over time, but still, it can complicate things.

Is there another option for email?

To address the downsides of third-party email clients, some MAM vendors offer a third alternative approach: They use the built-in email client, but protect attachments by encrypting them so that only corporate apps can open them. This requires some sort of proxy to do the actual attachment interception and encryption, and it also requires that the user has the apps that can open the attachments.

This middle-of-the-road technique still leaves contacts, calendars, tasks, and the clipboard accessible to third-party apps, but for a lot of companies, as long as the attachments are protected, this is good enough. (Remember with iOS, it's also possible to prevent messages from being forwarded using another email account, and other apps can be blocked from using the corporate account to send messages, so that helps, too.) You'll also need MDM to put password and encryption policies in place around the entire device.

Clearly, there are some compromises with this encrypted attachment approach, but that's just the reality of dealing with mobile email—all of the techniques require some compromise or another. This isn't the last time we'll talk about email and this compromise, either—it'll come up again a few more times throughout the rest of the book.

Mobile File Syncing

Beyond email (and the related contacts and calendaring), file sharing and syncing is probably the most important app that IT provides to users on mobile devices. Users have been accessing network share drives and folders for years, but when they picked up the iPhone and started to use it to do real work, a big problem was that there was no way to get their corporate shared files on it. (After all, there's no "net use" or "map a network drive" feature in iOS.)

So what happened? Hello Dropbox! (Or Box. Or Skydrive. Or Google Drive. Or SugarSync. Or, or, or...) Users love Dropbox, since they can install a simple agent on their desktop or laptop and then have access to all of their files from everywhere—including their mobile devices. And once those files are on their mobile devices, they can use the offline sync feature to store them on their devices or the "open in" functionality to get the files into whatever mobile app they want.

Needless to say, Dropbox is a problem for IT pros because it uses the cloud as its file storage location, and if users provision their own accounts, there's no way to secure or have any control over what they do with their files.

While users running off and getting their own Dropbox accounts is an IT pro's nightmare, fortunately there are dozens of "Dropbox for the enterprise"-type products in the world today. Many of these can run 100% on-premises (so you don't have to worry about storing data in the cloud) and have robust management policies and secure client apps. Products like Citrix ShareFile, VMware Horizon Data, AppSense DataNow, Watch-

Dox, Nomadesk, and others (many, many others) allow you to add Dropbox-like mobile file syncing functionality to all of your existing in-house file shares with in-house software. This combines the best of mobile file syncing and corporate controls, all without the cloud!

Mobile file syncing options

Most of these corporate mobile file syncing products include all the general management features we talked about in the chapter on MAM. So for your corporate files, these products provide encryption, password protection, remote wiping, app-level VPNs—all the good stuff.

Offline controls and sharing permissions are especially important. Policies that prevent users from saving or accessing files when a device is offline can be enforced, so that documents may not actually be store locally.

For document sharing, it's easy to implement policies that prevent users from opening documents into other applications. If you want to have *granular* controls over which other apps are allowed to open documents, things get a little more complicated. To have a selective "open-in" feature, most file syncing apps require that the other apps are also managed using the same MAM platform, so that the sharing can take place in a way that's not accessible to other unmanaged apps.

There are a few file syncing apps that have options for selective sharing with unmanaged apps, but remember that even though you can limit which apps can open the files, once the files are out of the file syncing app, they're out of your control. (Who says the user can't simply use that approved third-party app as a bridge to then open the file in some unapproved app?)

Beyond just controlling how users can share files and providing basic document viewing capabilities, file syncing clients have been steadily gaining capabilities in the past year. For example, some products now have full document editing capabilities for Office documents and other common file types. This saves the user from having to save the document into some other app, edit it, and then save it back into the file syncing app. It also means one less corporate application to figure out and deploy using MAM. (And frankly, it also reflects a trend toward files being more closely associated with the applications that are used to manipulate them as opposed to standalone independent objects.)

Some vendors go further when it comes to mobile document security—with one example being WatchDox. WatchDox takes documents and renders custom images of them on its servers so that they can be opened only with the WatchDox client app, which is available as a native app for several different platforms. It can also watermark apps with users' personal information to discourage them from taking screenshots. (The idea is that if you watermark a document with the user's name or some other identifying information, it will be less likely that the user will want to use screenshots to extract data.) To edit documents, it offers remote desktop-based applications. Obviously, that means there's no offline editing, but of course there are always tradeoffs that need to be made between security and usability.

Overall, there's a huge variety of file syncing solutions available today, with many different options for securely accessing and manipulating corporate data.

Mobile file syncing and the cloud

Once the issue of document security on the mobile device is taken care of, the next big concern with enterprise file syncing products is on the other end—where are all these corporate files actually stored? The common objection is that companies don't want to move their corporate files into public clouds, or that moving massive amounts of data would be difficult, or that moving files would break all sorts of systems that rely on the existing file structures.

The good news is that all of these concerns are actually non-issues when it comes to mobile file syncing, because mobile file syncing apps have absolutely nothing to do with cloud-based file storage! Many mobile file syncing products can simply be plugged into existing local storage in a matter of minutes. All you have to do is pop a virtual appliance into your data center, configure it to connect to your existing file shares, configure the policies for the clients, and that's it. There's no need for a massively disruptive "move to the cloud." You can literally Dropbox-ify your existing file shares in a matter of minutes! So while many EMM products involve cloud-enabled software as a service, whether you implement "mobile file syncing" or "the cloud" are actually two completely separate decisions.

Does this mean that Dropbox is going away?

Does providing a corporate file syncing client mean that none of your users will ever install Dropbox again? No way! Instead, it means that users don't have to "break out" their corporate files to if they need them on a mobile device. The idea is that from a user's perspective, downloading and signing into a corporate file syncing app should be easier than figuring that they need to use Dropbox, setting up an account, paying money, installing an agent on their desktop, and installing the Dropbox mobile app.

Secure Mobile Browsers

The third core app for almost any MAM deployment is the web browser on a mobile device. Again, the value proposition here is the same as with MAM in general—you can put all the management controls directly in the corporate browser app instead of managing the entire device to put controls around the built-in browser. The best part about third-party browser apps on mobile devices is that most of them use the exact same rendering engines as the built-in browser, so the user won't notice any difference in the look, feel, and performance of websites. Only the "chrome" of the browser (the address bar, controls, and other elements that surround the page being displayed) will look different.

Corporate-managed mobile browsers are pretty simple, but powerful. Here's a basic list of what you can do:

- You can provide access to internal web apps and intranet sites without having to use MDM to connect the device to a VPN.

- Just like any other managed app, you can control how the clipboard and other sharing functions are used.
- Browsing can be limited to corporate-approved sites. (Let users visit all the questionable parts of the Internet from their own browsers.)
- You can provision bookmarks to corporate web apps.
- Web links from other managed apps can open in your chosen browser instead of the default browser. This is also a good way to get around the fact that iOS doesn't let you change the default browser.
- If the connection is tunneled to the corporate network, the browser can use the company's DNS.
- In Chapter 6, I mentioned hybrid apps: HTML5 apps that run inside of native browser shells. While many hybrid apps are distributed much like standalone native apps, corporate browsers can provide another distribution option.

9. Building a Corporate Ecosystem and Enabling Dual Persona

So far in this book we've traced the path of mobility from the BlackBerry days to unmanaged devices to MDM to dealing with dual persona, finally ending up on mobile app management. The next step after basic MAM is to bring all of these apps together to build a corporate app ecosystem.

Bringing All of Your Managed Apps Together

What exactly are we talking about when we say "creating a corporate app ecosystem?" For this I mean gathering all the managed apps on a mobile device, enabling them to talk to one another, enabling them to plug into the corporate resources, and figuring out what their relationship with the device and personal apps will be.

This is where mobile app management really comes together—all the management features that IT needs are in place without severely impacting the user experience for the rest of the device.

What's this corporate app ecosystem like for the user? Users have a collection of work apps for all of their basic tasks. Getting into these apps will probably require a password, but once they're in, the apps flow smoothly into one another as needed. A link from an email opens right into the corporate browser, which logs directly onto the corporate network. Documents from the file syncing client open directly into the appropriate corporate apps. Text can be pasted into work apps but not out. Ordinary documents can be synced locally and opened offline, but more sensitive documents might be view-only and require the device to be online. Users are already familiar with the way applications call each other back and forth (look at the way the Gmail iOS app can open links directly into Chrome, for example). The work app icons can be intermingled with the rest of the user's apps, or they can be hidden away in a folder. Work apps can send the user notifications, or they can be turned off for evenings and weekends. There can be a corporate app store that directs users to the company's offerings of other managed apps, or the user might be able to head directly to public app stores and find compatible apps. Is the device managed? It's much less relevant at this point. For the most part for users, "work" is just a collection of a few apps, and users can interact with those apps as they please.

The overall experience is quite the opposite from that terrible experience described in the beginning of Chapter 5. Now, using a device for work can mean that an ecosystem of corporate apps rides on top of what's already there. It doesn't mean that the entire device experience changes.

This is dual persona mobile app management.

Dealing with the phone number

One of the interesting things that comes up when talking about combining work and personal into a single phone is what do you do about the actual phone number?

An advantage of having two devices is that users can leave their work phone at home on evenings and weekends when they want to disconnect from work. But if you use this dual persona stuff to combine both work and personal on a single device, does that now mean that users are accessible by phone 24/7? (Sure, most of us have personal phone numbers for our employees so we can call them in an emergency, but if their work phone numbers are tied to mobile phones that are with them 24/7, you run into a lot of situations where people will accidentally call an employee after hours just because they didn't know they were calling someone at home!)

This is a big deal, actually, and the lack of separate work and personal phone numbers has been a big issue preventing many people from wanting a single phone. It's definitely something you have to deal with.

A few years ago, there was this fantasy that we'd soon see phones that had two SIM cards in them, so a single device could have two different phone numbers (and two different data plans). While there are a few phones with dual SIM card support, these are not mainstream at all.

One of the best ways to handle the "two phone numbers on one phone" problem is with some type of newer office phone system, many of which have softphone client apps, VoIP, and user-configurable call forwarding. Pretty much all the big corporate phone systems now have apps for mobile devices that you (or your users) can use to control how and when their work numbers ring their personal phones. Some of these use the actual voice connection to the phones, while others use VoIP via dedicated apps. Many of these products also have dialers users can use to replace the built-in dialer (which itself is just an app). So if users are making work calls, they use the work dialer, and if they're making personal calls, they use the phone's built-in dialer app.

Other users choose to take this into their own hands. I personally have a single mobile phone with my personal phone number on it, but I also have a Google Voice account. I give out the Google Voice phone number as my "work" number, meaning I can control when (and if) it rings through to my mobile phone or not. And if I want to make outbound calls that show the caller ID as coming from my work number instead of my personal number, I just use the Google Voice dialer app instead of the one that came with my phone.

What happens when you combine MDM with a MAM ecosystem?

We haven't been talking about MDM for the past few chapters, and certainly one of the great things about MAM is that it can function in the absence of device-level management. However, when MDM is combined with MAM, there are naturally more management options. And to be clear, I'm talking specifically about what happens when you include iOS configuration profiles or use the Android Device Administration API in addition to app-level controls.

Here's what you can get when you mix MDM and MAM:

- First, there's more visibility into the device, like which apps are installed or information about the hardware.
- There can be multiple layers of security—for example, two passwords to get through before users get to the sensitive data.
- For iOS (and some versions of Android), you'll be able to install and remove apps.
- If you're using native email, you'll need MDM to at least put some basic policies on the device.

Aside from these basics, one of the more interesting things you can do when combining MDM and MAM is to use the state of the device to inform app management policies. For example, if a device is managed and has a password, corporate apps might not need to have a password. Naturally, for policies like these, your MDM and MAM have to be able to work together.

The end of the MAM versus MDM debate?

There are certainly a lot of different ways to mix MDM and MAM together (and Chapter 11 will cover more specific scenarios). The interesting thing is that it was only recently (in late 2012 and early 2013) that the EMM industry got to a point where most vendors have both MDM and MAM capabilities. This wasn't always the case—for a while, upstart MAM vendors were almost in a battle with MDM vendors. Today, we can still debate "MDM versus MAM" and the best way to deal with devices, but it doesn't have to be a "vendor versus vendor" argument. This is great because it allows companies to focus a lot more on their management needs and less on which acronym they want to pick.

How do you integrate all this EMM stuff with everything else you do in IT?

Throughout this whole book, we've been looking at enterprise mobility management purely in the context of managing apps and mobile devices. But of course mobile apps and devices don't live in their own isolated silos—they actually need to be integrated with all of the other IT systems and services that you provide. So how do you hook the two together?

First and foremost, most EMM solutions integrate with Active Directory, so there's no need to build databases of users and groups from scratch. Some EMM solutions can even be driven through other management systems, through APIs, or via components that connect with Microsoft System Center Configuration Manager or Symantec Altiris Client Management Suite. (Basically, whatever you use to manage users, devices, and application access in your enterprise today, there's probably an MDM product that can hook right into that. You just have to look for it.)

The list of integration possibilities goes on. Many EMM products incorporate network access control, VPNs, unified communications, telecom expense management, DLP (data loss prevention), collaboration suites, app analytics, and Windows-based virtual desktop access. Again, if you're using it and it's important to your enterprise, there's probably an EMM vendor out there that can extend whatever you have to your mobile devices.

The thing to keep in mind is that the vendors offering EMM solutions today come from a wide range of backgrounds. There are startups that deal exclusively with mobile devices, there are companies that have been around for years, there are enormous systems management vendors, and there are desktop virtualization and application delivery vendors. Like many other situations, picking your EMM solution is going to be a choice between pure-play dedicated vendors and larger, more integrated offerings.

How Are We Supposed to Get All of These Apps?

This ecosystem of managed apps sounds great, doesn't it? But you're probably thinking, "Wait, how are we supposed to get all of these managed apps again?" I talked about the basic underlying techniques back in Chapter 7, but now I want to look at MAM again from the real-world perspective of actually trying to acquire all of these apps and bring them together into a corporate ecosystem.

Now of course the vast majority of apps out there don't work with MAM, but when you put it in context, that's okay. This book isn't about strategies around which apps to mobilize or anything like that, but the point is that obviously you don't need a managed corporate version of every single app out there. And within the narrower context of corporate applications, building a MAM environment doesn't mean you have to figure out how to mobilize every one of your applications before you get started. There are some easy basic places to start, like email, file syncing, and managed browsers. Once you get the basics down, you can gradually bring more apps into the fold as needed.

MAM techniques in the real world

Remember that there are four basic sources for MAM-compatible apps:

- Apps from MAM vendors.
- In-house apps built to MAM specifications.
- App wrapping to modify pre-built apps.
- ISVs that partner with MAM vendors.

(The fifth option, client apps that are managed through whatever SaaS product they're associated with, won't be mentioned here, since we're assuming that this class of apps already has whatever relevant management features are needed.)

The important underlying fact to know is that MAM apps work only with the management platform they were built to work with. While there are a few apps out there that have open APIs that can be addressed by different management platforms, the apps that we're talking about here work only with the MAM platform that they were specifically created to work with.

Apps from MAM vendors

The easiest way to get manageable apps is to go directly to MAM vendors. Many of them already provide the basic apps, and it's great because they just work, they can be tightly integrated with one another and the management platform, and they're usually free once you've bought into the MAM product.

This is great in concept, though in the real world, sometimes the apps that the EMM vendors write or license are horrible. It's kind of funny that an EMM vendor can be great at building an awesome management console with tons of flexible policies and back-end integration, but bad at creating apps that end users actually like. In fact, for this reason, many EMM vendors completely stay out of the app-making business, especially for email apps where the limitations inherent in iOS make things difficult. Of course on the other hand, some EMM vendors actually take the time to make totally cool apps with tons of extra valuable features—really it all just depends on your vendor.

One of the challenges this can cause is a "tail wagging the dog" scenario where you might be forced to use a certain app just because your EMM vendor chooses to use it. You could use one of the other MAM techniques to use apps from other vendors, but then the integration might not be as good.

In-house apps

If your company is building an in-house app (or having somebody build it for you), then making sure it's compatible with MAM is easy. It's simply a matter of using an SDK from your MAM provider. This, too, can be hit or miss, depending on your MAM product. Some of them are as simple as adding one single line of code to your app when you're writing it, while others might require major architectural changes to your app's source code. (Then of course MAM vendors that offer "wrapping" instead of SDKs argue that SDKs are hard to use and that just wrapping the compiled app is the way to go.) The takeaway is that if you know that you want to manage an in-house or custom app with a given MAM product, it shouldn't be hard to do.

App wrapping pre-built apps

If you'd like to use your MAM vendor's app wrapping capabilities to wrap existing apps from established ISVs, things get more complicated, because now you have to deal with factors like licensing and Apple's esoteric restrictions.

Remember that with app wrapping, there's this idea that if there's an app out there you want to manage, you go directly to the app's creator and ask for a copy (because of course you can't wrap apps directly from public app stores). You strike some sort of agreement, the creator sends you the app binary, you run it through your app wrapping tool, and then finally you sign it yourself and distribute it as an enterprise app. While it sounds fairly straightforward in theory, there are several unanswered questions that come up.

First off, what's that conversation with the app creator going to be like? Even I really have only anecdotal evidence here: On one hand, it seems completely implausible that you could go to the creator of any significantly successful app and not be laughed out of the room when you ask to do your own distribution of the app. On the other hand, there are MAM vendors that say yes, many smaller ISVs are willing to do special app wrapping deals. I guess it depends on who you talk to at the ISV and how much competition it has. (Or how hungry it is to sell licenses.)

The other much larger problem is that this model doesn't seem to actually be compliant with Apple's rules for app distribution. According to most interpretations, doing an enterprise in-house distribution of an app that's already available in the public Apple App Store isn't allowed. And the evidence seems to suggest that Apple doesn't view a wrapped version of an app different enough from the original app to consider it a completely separate app.

Another way that some ISVs and corporate customers are doing app wrapping is to not even have a public version of an app at all—instead, both parties bypass the Apple App Store entirely. ISVs distribute apps directly to customers, who then sign and distribute them to their employees using their own iOS Developer Enterprise Program certificates. Again, this is something that Apple doesn't really like. If an app is aimed at a wide audience, it wants it to be in the public Apple App Store.

The Apple B2B program provides some more options, though typical for Apple, the rules still aren't completely clear. The wording with the B2B program indicates that it's okay to use it to distribute apps that are just slightly modified versions of public apps, so app wrapping would be okay. The problem is that B2B apps are really supposed to be targeted only at individual companies, not all the companies that happen to be using a certain MAM platform.

Underlying this whole conversation is the fear that Apple could take away either the right of an ISV or the right of a company to distribute apps at any time. There are plenty of stories about Apple shutting down smaller developers or pulling apps. However, none of the MAM vendors I've spoken to in the past couple of years has ever heard of Apple revoking a company's iOS Developer Enterprise Program account.

Publicly available apps

The obvious solution to all of this is to simply have MAM capabilities built into the publicly distributed versions of apps. This certainly avoids a lot of messiness, but there are still some issues here. First and foremost is the fact that whether a public version of an app is written to work with a particular MAM product is up to the ISV and the MAM vendor, not you.

Some ISVs have multiple versions of their apps publicly available in the Apple App Store, so there's the normal version and then the MAM-compatible version. But again, Apple's preference is for there to be just one version of an app—having a normal version and a MAM version of an app doesn't make them different enough to qualify as separate apps. (Despite this, you can find plenty of apps today that do this exact thing, which is more evidence of the somewhat arbitrary application of Apple's app policies.) In a perfect world, MAM functionality would lie latent in the app until it gets activated, so one version of an app would work in all situations, but again, that's up to the app maker, not us.

This public distribution model seems to be the best option, except we still have to deal with the fact that apps built for MAM have to be built for a specific MAM platform. There are about a dozen vendors out there today that all offer fairly similar MAM capabilities, but you can't take an app built for one platform and manage it with another.

You can imagine how annoying this gets. MAM vendors are in a race to sign on partner ISVs to incorporate their SDKs. But for end-user customers wanting to use apps with MAM, buying into a MAM vendor could mean buying into its ecosystem of apps. Then what happens when the app your users demand isn't compatible with your MAM platform?

There are some ISVs that work with multiple MAM vendors, and sometimes they simply have multiple versions of their app in the public app store (so it would be "App X," "App X, MAM vendor Y edition," and "App X, MAM vendor Z edition"). This is cool for now but ultimately unsustainable and confusing, not to mention that Apple doesn't like it. The other option is for ISVs to incorporate multiple different MAM SDKs into a single app, but this can get tricky, too. Building in a bunch of SDKs can take up a lot of space, not to mention that it adds more time to the development process.

Clearly there's a need for some sort of industry wide standard for mobile app management APIs that could be used by every app maker. This standard could be formal (in fact, at the time of the writing of this book, MobileIron was starting to talk about an effort called the Open App Alliance), or it could be just de facto (through acquisitions, OEM agreements, licensing, or natural market forces). Either way, having some sort of standards for MAM would help users, ISVs, and MAM vendors. But none exist yet. (Check out my blog on BrianMadden.com for the latest on this, as seeing this happen is sort of a "pet project" of mine.)

The lesson from all of this is that your choice of EMM vendor could have a significant impact on what apps are available to you to manage. Apple's review guidelines could change, too. Talk to your vendor, and good luck.

Conclusion

Despite the need for standards and more guidance from Apple (and, to a lesser extent, Google), mobile app management (with publicly available apps) is one of the best ways we have to enable dual persona and create ecosystems of corporate apps.

The changes coming to iOS 7 may change the MAM conversation a bit, especially for select features. However, there's nothing that indicates that there are nearly enough new features to fully enable dual persona, so we'll still need MAM for that.

And for Android, fragmentation means that we have to be able to deal with the lowest common denominator. As long as we face these challenges, and as long as companies want to provide their users with native mobile access to data and applications, mobile app management will be important.

10. Dealing with BYOD

So far we haven't spent too much time talking about BYOD, even though I'll bet about half of you reading this book picked it up specifically because you wanted to know about BYOD! But now that we've spent a few hundred pages talking about MDM, MAM, and EMM, we can finally circle around and throw users back into the conversation again.

If you've actually read everything up to this point, you know that from a "technical" perspective, BYOD doesn't matter. That is to say that whether a device is owned by the company or by the employee doesn't really affect the options you have to manage it. All the technologies, techniques, and products we've covered apply to "mobile devices," not "personal devices" or "work devices."

And remember, don't be fooled into thinking you can prevent BYOD by buying company phones and locking them down like crazy. Your employees will still bring in their own personal devices, and you'll have all the same issues to deal with again. So you might as well figure out how to make this dual persona thing work for all scenarios, BYOD or not!

All that said, I understand that BYOD is a big deal to a lot of different companies (and for a lot of different reasons). And even though you might know that BYOD doesn't really matter from a technical standpoint, that doesn't really help you when the CIO is breathing down your neck demanding that you create a BYOD policy. So let's look at important issues for considering BYOD versus corporate-owned devices and various options for addressing them.

What Is BYOD Really?

BYOD. Bring your own device. Obviously you know what the term means, but how BYOD works in a practical sense is different to everyone. Ask 10 different people to explain what BYOD is and you'll get 10 different answers. Let's take a look at some of the possibilities of what BYOD could mean:

- The company gets out of the business of buying mobile devices and paying phone bills. Employees buy their own phones and bring them in.
- The company supplies the mobile devices, but users "own" the rights to do whatever they want with them.
- Users buy whatever devices they want, but the company still pays the monthly bill. (This is what we do at TechTarget, the company where I work.)
- The company buys the mobile devices and pays for the airtime, but users still bring in their own extra things. (This happens a lot. The company provides and pays for mobile phones, but users bring in their own iPads.)
- The company provides locked-down devices and bans BYOD, so users bring in their own stuff without telling anyone from IT.

- The company lets users do whatever they want, but provides them with a monthly stipend for the phone bill to help offset expenses (for example, the company gives each employee a mobile phone reimbursement of $50 per month in their paycheck).
- The company allows users to bring whatever they want, but tells them that if they want corporate apps on their phones, they must bring a certain device (for example, if you want corporate email on your phone, it has to be an iPhone 4 or newer, Android 4.0 or newer, or a BlackBerry 7 or newer).

Really I could go on and on. None of these scenarios is right or wrong or "true" BYOD—it's just that BYOD means different things to different people. (By the way, this is a double-edged sword! On one hand, if your boss wants you to "do BYOD," you can just pick one of the easy options and do it! On the other hand, your boss may have some crazy notion of what BYOD is and your job implementing it could be pretty miserable.)

What BYOD really means depends on your environment

The biggest thing that will impact what BYOD means is the culture—both the company culture and where you are in the world. For example, some companies may have users who are super-sensitive to employee privacy. At other companies, the relationship between IT and employees is completely dysfunctional and users are unwilling to give up any management of "their" devices. There's also a big difference between "voluntary BYOD" (Yay! We can use iPhones now!) and "forced BYOD" (Dammit! Our cheap company is screwing us by making us buy our own phones now!).

Coming from San Francisco, I obviously like the type of BYOD where the company is saying, "Yes, we respect that you all want to work in different ways and with different devices, so we want to support that." That's my kind of BYOD!

On the other hand, imagine a company that decides one day to stop providing corporate devices and instead requires employees to use their personal devices. The company might think, "Hey, this BYOD thing is popular now. Let's do it!" But in this case, it's not doing BYOD at all! The company is just offloading costs and asking employees to pay their own phone bills. If a company does this and then puts restrictions on how employees use their devices, then it might as well have given everyone a pay cut. Meanwhile, the company gets covered in the county business journal as being cool and progressive with its "BYOD" program.

This is clearly no fun for employees and is not the point of BYOD. A real effort to accommodate BYOD takes into account that users may want to do work from a wide variety of devices, some of them corporate-owned, many of them not. If a user voluntarily brings in a personal device, then yes, he or she might have to agree to some sort of management policies for that device. But overall, there's nothing anyone can do to stop the flood of personal devices.

(Okay, if you really want to be in control of every single endpoint that every user has to access corporate resources and completely eliminate BYOD, all you have to do is issue every user several phones, multiple tablets, a stack of computers, and a wireless 4G card. Oh, and do this every three months, and put metal detectors around the office doors to make sure no unauthorized devices come in!)

But seriously, keep in mind that BYOD is actually about device ownership, not device management, and you'll be fine.

Can You Save Money with BYOD?

One of the big drivers with BYOD is financial, as many companies believe they're going to save money with BYOD. "All of our users already have personal iPhones," they think, "so why should we be buying them second devices? Let's just 'let' them use their personal ones and save the money!"

So does BYOD save money? It depends on what you believe, what you *want* to believe, and how you conduct your analysis. If you read the introduction to this book, you know that I co-authored *The VDI Delusion* in 2012 with Brian Madden and Gabe Knuth. In that book, we had a whole chapter called "How to Lie with Cost Models" (which itself was based on an article Brian wrote a few years prior). We argued that when it comes to IT cost savings, you can make the results of your analysis "prove" whatever you want. And typically the point that's "proven" is whatever you already believed moving into your analysis. I won't go into all the details of this here—just Google it—but I will provide a few examples around alleged costs savings of moving to BYOD.

The main problem with the "savings" of BYOD is that you're not actually reducing the amount of money that is spent on mobile phones and monthly bills—you're just transferring the costs from the company to the employee. If you're going to make employees buy their own $400 phone every other year and then pay for only half of their monthly phone bill, how's that any different from charging for parking in the employee lot or making employees pay for the electricity they use in their cubicles?

You also have to deal with the fact that some employees really don't like to spend money. So everyone may have had Android or iPhones or BlackBerrys back when you were buying them, but now that you make the employees buy them, are they really going to buy that $400 enterprise-grade smartphone, or are they going to take the free Android 2.3 device that the carrier has on clearance? If the employees lose productivity because they can't access all of their stuff, are you really saving money, or are you losing money?

Every company I know that tried to "convert" to BYOD always ended up screwing some employees in some ways, and in the end, I just have to wonder if it's worth it. For example, I have a friend who works at a big company that recently decided to "go BYOD." The company sent an email to all employees saying, "Starting next week, no more work phones. You can either use your existing personal phone or we will transfer your existing work phone to you personally, and then we will reimburse you $50 per month for your work-related activities on your personal phone." The problem was that my friend had just bought a new iPhone from Verizon (which was not a global phone at the time). So if she took the company work phone to replace her iPhone, she'd have to pay the $350 early termination fee for her iPhone. But if she kept the iPhone, she couldn't use it outside of the U.S. She ultimately decided to keep the iPhone, but now when she travels to international events, she doesn't have a mobile phone, which surely costs the company more lost value in productivity than if it had just bought her an international phone. (Which it wouldn't do, because hey, it was doing BYOD to save money!)

Working With Personal "Consumer" Devices

One of the biases that's ingrained into many IT professionals is that employees bring in these "consumer" devices (said with disdain) that are not appropriate for "real work." After all, doesn't everything have to be tested by IT so that only certified devices and configurations can go on the corporate network? That is certainly a problem for PCs and laptops, where specifications between corporate laptops and the $399 special actually matter, and supporting a cheap laptop can be a huge pain. But for mobile devices, this is a lot different.

Obviously for Apple devices, this isn't a problem—there are a limited number of different hardware configurations, and it's easy to keep the OS up to date.

But what about Android? Aside from the OS fragmentation issues that we've been talking about throughout the book, there are thousands of different hardware configurations from hundreds of different manufacturers. That means there's a lot of cheap crap out there. Some of these sub-$100 tablets may be painfully slow, but that's not really our problem—we care more about the OS. The good news is that today it's pretty hard to find anything for sale that has an OS older than Android 2.3, and most everything that you can buy new in a store or from a carrier these days has Android 4.0, 4.1, or 4.2. And remember that relying more on

MAM than on MDM is probably the best way to deal with those older OSes.

Honestly, the biggest concern is going to be users of the Kindle Fire, Barnes & Noble Nook, and other devices that can't interact with the Google Play ecosystem. Some cheap devices break or completely omit important features like the Device Administration API, and getting corporate apps installed could be a hassle. There are a few EMM vendors that do have apps in alternative marketplaces, but certainly not enough to rely on.

All of these obscure devices are probably going to create a situation where you have to say no to supporting them. But is that really much of a problem? Setting a minimum device requirement—say, Android 2.2, the ability to access the Google Play ecosystem, and the ability to sideload in-house apps if needed—is probably reasonable. The user's management options and degree of access may vary depending on OS version or whether custom MDM APIs are present, but the bottom line is that EMM technology today can deal with the vast majority of "consumer" devices.

"But users will just break their personal junk, and then I'll have to support it!"

Another fear about BYOD is what happens when devices are broken or out of service? In the past, you've always been responsible for providing support. Users break it and you fix it. So in this BYOD world of users running who knows what, how does support work?

Quite frankly, support for user-owned devices is really no different from the way that support has worked for years. The only difference is that if users break something on their own device, they have to go back to the Apple store or wherever they bought it to get it fixed. In the meantime, if they can't get a temporary device from their repair shop, they can always get a loaner from you, which ought to be easy to set up because you're using EMM.

Is that as ideal as supporting only one single device that all users have? Of course not. But it's the reality of today, like it or not.

One of the common objections to this general approach is along the lines of, "It's the job of corporate IT to provide a functional computing environment for my users. If they have to go all the way across town to the Apple store to get their phone fixed, then we're dealing with several hours of lost productivity, which wouldn't happen if we just gave them all company phones."

While I empathize with the sentiment behind this argument, I just don't believe it's relevant today. In today's world, we trust our employees to do all sorts of things on their own. A hundred years ago, most employees worked in big factories and got to work each day in company-provided buses. Then at some point individual employees wanted more freedom and started driving their own cars to work. I'm sure somewhere along the line, some mid-level manager argued, "Our employees don't know how to maintain their own automobiles! If we let them drive to work, what happens if they run out of petroleum distillate or forget to revulcanize their tires? They will break down and be hours late for work. We cannot allow this risk!"

And how did that turn out? We pretty much all get ourselves to work each day. Sure, sometimes bad days happen and we lose a few hours of productivity because we do something stupid like blow out a tire we neglected to maintain or put gas in our diesel engine. But overall, we manage to get ourselves to work most of the time and our companies are no longer in the employee transportation business.

The same is true for devices. Yeah, a few employees might lose a little bit of time here and there due to personal device failures, but overall, lost productivity will be minimal, and it's certainly not a reason to try to stop BYOD.

A quick note about tablets

Much like everything else in this book, all this talk about BYOD applies equally to tablets and phones, since managing Android and iOS is identical regardless of how large the device's screen is. Ordinarily, I wouldn't even bring this up because I'm sure you know it by now, but unfortunately, this tablet conversation comes up in the context of BYOD because there are still a lot of companies that treat phones and tablets differently. Some companies believe that while mobile phones have been essential for a decade or two, tablets are still a "luxury" item or an auxiliary tool. They might think, "We will buy phones for users because those are essential, but if employees want to use tablets, they have to buy them themselves." While that's a perfectly valid position to take, make sure you don't slip into the mindset of "we will 'allow' users to bring in phones, but not tablets," as this doesn't really make sense from a technical standpoint.

The pride-of-ownership effect

We've spent enough time in this book talking about how you can safely provide corporate apps and data on users' devices alongside personal stuff, so hopefully you're on board with that as a concept. One of the other fascinating facets of this decision is something called the "pride of ownership" effect.

Put simply, the pride-of-ownership effect means that users are more careful, respectful, and "proud" of a device that has "their" stuff on it. This manifests itself in many ways. The simplest is if users leave their phone in a cab or at a restaurant, for example, and the phone is full of their photos and other personal stuff, they'll probably want to run back and track it down. But if it's "just" a work phone, they're more likely to think, "Pfft... I'll just call the helpdesk and get a replacement tomorrow." So overall, "personal" devices (or devices that at least feel personal) are lost less often than corporate devices.

The pride-of-ownership effect also has the potential to affect security. While users might not care about strangers accessing their corporate information on a lost device, they're likely to be careful and have a password with a device that's full of their personal information and photos. (Though that's not always the case: A quick poll of my co-workers in our San Francisco office showed that about 50% of them do not have passcodes on their phones, despite having personal email, photos, and Facebook available on them!)

Finally, the pride-of-ownership phenomena means that users tend to call the helpdesk less often to fix simple issues. There's this idea that they will figure out how to fix things on their own because they don't want IT messing with "their" phone. So you end up with the helpdesk being the last resort instead of the first resort.

Why BYOD Ultimately Doesn't Matter

I've hinted a few times throughout this book that in many ways, BYOD doesn't actually matter. Sure, it may matter to you when your boss says, "Figure out how to do BYOD!" But in terms of actual technology, you have to figure out how to manage and secure the mobile devices that access your apps and data regardless of who actually pays for them. From that point, BYOD is much more of an issue for human resources and lawyers than for IT. (We'll come back to this later on.)

And there's one other note on BYOD that's worth mentioning. Several analyst-type people have recently started throwing around the acronym COPE, which stands for corporate-owned, personally enabled. The idea is that devices the company owns are treated the same as personal devices, using whatever mixture of management techniques and apps is appropriate. Again, this underscores the idea that device ownership and management policies are two separate things, and this whole notion of COPE isn't a big deal and certainly shouldn't surprise anyone who's read this book up to this point.

11. Putting It All Together: Deployment Considerations for EMM

We've spent 150 pages looking at all the details of how MDM and MAM work. This chapter is going to look at all the different ways that these technologies can be used and combined.

Deployment Variables

First, there are several things you have to figure out regardless of how you're going to use MDM and MAM. Before we look at the different deployment scenarios, consider these variables:

Email

Remember that email is probably the No. 1 enterprise app for most companies and users. Also remember that there are many different technical options for making email work on devices. (Are you going to use the native built-in client? Are you going to use the native client with a solution that encrypts attachments to prevent them from leaking? Are you going to use a third-party email app provided by your EMM vendor?)

Device management

By now you know that there's a big different between device-level (MDM) and app-level (MAM) security and management. So as you're moving forward with your planning, you have to think about how tight you want the security to be on your actual devices. Do you want no device-level security (instead using MAM to protect only your corporate apps)? Do you want four-digit passcodes? Or do you want complex passwords that expire once a month?

Personal apps

Next think about whether you will give your users the ability to install their own apps. If so, will they be able to install any apps they want, or only ones that you pre-approve? If you decide that, how will you decide which apps will be approved?

Also keep in mind from the last chapter that you need to make this decision regardless of whether you have corporate-owned or user-owned devices. Of course you could decide that you'll allow different things based on who owns the device. Maybe you'll only allow apps from the official Google Play store on your corporate-owned Android devices, but you'll allow apps from anywhere on user-own devices. Or you might decide that you won't allow user-installed apps on shared iPads, but iPads that are assigned to particular employees will allow users to install whatever they want.

Corporate apps

Next think about what corporate apps you're going to provide to your users. In addition to email, calendars, and contacts, will you provide file syncing? Office editing tools? A managed browser? Other enterprise apps?

Corporate MAM ecosystem

Finally, think about the "ecosystem" of all the corporate apps that you'd like to provide. Do you want all the various corporate apps to be able to communicate with each other (cut, copy, and paste, "Open In," data sharing, etc.)? Do you want to enable single sign-on so users just authenticate to one corporate app and then they can use all the corporate apps without signing in again?

Example Deployment Scenarios

After you've decided how you're going to handle all the basic components of EMM in your environment, your next step is to think about how you'll design your mix of MDM and MAM tools. When you look at the options for different policies, you can see that there's a whole range of possible combinations. We can break that range of combinations into six main scenarios. (And again, remember that you might go with different options for various subsets of users or devices.)

The options are:

- MDM alone with locked-down policies
- MDM alone with light policies
- MDM and MAM with built-in email
- MDM and MAM with encrypted email attachments
- MDM and MAM with a third-party email client
- MAM alone

Let's dig into each of these one by one.

MDM alone with locked-down policies

This scenario is using MDM to do just device-level management, with no MAM-compatible apps. Email is synced to the built-in client, and to protect it, users are restricted in their ability to install apps. (Hence, the "locked-down policies" part.)

Pros:

- Not much goes on with this device that IT doesn't know about or control. MDM policies determine network and VPN access, set tight security policies, and keep track of all the apps that get installed on the device.
- This approach works well for devices that are used by multiple users as a secondary or single-task device. For example: public kiosks, tablets that take the place of embedded devices, iPads used as cash registers, badge and ticket scanners, or thin clients.
- This approach can be used for corporate-owned devices in highly regulated industries.

Cons:

- The usability might not be great, thanks to long passwords and the like.
- Nobody wants to have this done to their personal device.
- Blacklisting apps isn't always a smooth process.
- If you're using iOS and the solution you choose doesn't utilize an agent app, there's a chance the device could be jailbroken without you knowing it.
- Aside from email and web app access, MDM alone doesn't actually provide access to corporate resources.
- Capabilities on Android devices will vary due to fragmentation.

MDM alone with light policies

Like the previous option, this option is based around using MDM with just email delivered via the built-in client and no other MAM-compatible apps. The difference here is that you're using MDM to just deliver the basics, and otherwise users can do whatever they want with their devices.

Pros:

- Users like it because they can install whatever apps they want and the overall experience isn't that different from using an unmanaged device.
- Corporate policies set up Wi-Fi, VPNs, and email access, so users don't have to figure out how to do all this on their own.
- There's not really too much to actively monitor or worry about. You just set your policies and provision your settings and users are ready to go.
- This can be viewed as a simple "autoconfiguration" of new devices without any heavy-handed management. Even if a company decided it doesn't want EMM at all, using MDM for basic device configuration saves IT a lot of time.

Cons:

- User-installed apps can easily leak corporate data.
- Again, aside from email and web app access, MDM alone doesn't actually provide access to corporate resources.

MDM and MAM with built-in email

This scenario adds some MAM capabilities to the device-level MDM management. Email and other PIM apps still leverage all the built-in apps on the device.

Pros:

- Corporate apps on the device can make it more useful for getting actual work done.
- The user gets a completely native email experience.

Cons:

- Corporate data in the built-in email app is still susceptible to leaking via personal apps.

MDM and MAM with encrypted email attachments

This option is just like the previous one that leverages MDM, MAM, and the built-in email apps, with the difference being that you use an email solution that encrypts attachments so they can be used only by corporate-approved apps that are able to decrypt them.

Pros:

- The best of both worlds—users get built-in email, yet corporate attachments are secured.

Cons:

- This requires some sort of back-end proxy or agent to do the attachment encryption.
- Corporate apps have to be specially built to work with the encrypted attachments.
- Email text, contacts, calendars, contacts, and tasks are still exposed to personal apps.

MDM and MAM with third-party email client

The next option to consider is MDM with MAM where you also use a third-party sandboxed email app instead of the one that comes built into the device. In this case, most of your corporate data and files stay within the protected ecosystem of apps.

Pros:

- Email, contacts, and calendars are all protected.
- Device management can provide a redundant layer of management, ensuring corporate data outside of the managed apps is still protected.
- MDM can be used to install the apps.

Cons:

- Users might dislike the email client.
- All of the work apps have to be compatible with each other.

MAM alone

The final option is to just use MAM and not worry about device management or MDM. In this case, everything work-related is in a managed app. Built-in apps or user-installed apps cannot access corporate resources unless allowed by policy. The device itself is not managed.

Pros:

- It's a simple concept: You use work apps to do work, just like any service.
- If the apps are managed correctly, it shouldn't matter what personal apps are on the device.
- There's absolutely no impact to the usability of the personal side of the device. Users can hide all the work apps in a folder and ignore them when they're not working.
- This is good for devices that are only occasionally used for work.
- IT doesn't have to worry about what's going on with the rest of the device.

Cons:

- IT might have to figure out how to deploy many different apps. Where are these going to come from?
- You might have to jump through some hoops to make sure that all of your apps can work together in the MAM environment.
- IT doesn't have visibility about what's going on with the rest of the device. (Notice that this is also listed under pros.)

Deployment Considerations

Now that we've stepped through all of these options, you've probably already thought of plenty of ways that you can use them in your environment. However, the point of all of this isn't to go down the list and pick out a management technology—it's really just for reference.

The first step should be to consider what services you need to deliver to your users and what the minimum security requirements are—and then figure out the most user-friendly way to do it. Deciding on a management technology before figuring out what users really need leads to all those unpleasant situations we talked about in Chapter 5.

Having said that, to a significant degree, we can condense the whole conversation down to one question: How will you handle email (and calendars and contacts)? The reason should be pretty clear by now: For file syncing and any other enterprise apps, you have to provide a mobile app no matter what, and when you're providing an app, you can easily manage it. But with email, there's the option to use the built-in app or not use the built-in app. As you saw in the previous section (and in Chapter 8), the choice for email has a big impact on the user experience, and unfortunately, there's a compromise somewhere, on someone's part, no matter what.

It's all about compromise

It's more than just email that requires a compromise, though—it's all of EMM. Think about it: If you want corporate data to reside on personal devices and still have it be controlled by policies, something in the experience is going to have to give somewhere, whether it's adding a passcode, preventing users from accessing corporate data from unapproved apps, or forcing users to use some obscure mail client they might not like.

It's the same tradeoff that has been around forever: security versus ease of use. The most easy-to-use device is one that has corporate email in the built-in client, no password, and whatever apps the user wants to install. The most secure device has a long, complex password, a third-party email client, and no user-installed apps. (Well, really it should also be powered off and buried in concrete, but let's be practical.) The reality is that it's impossible for a device to be 100% secure and 100% easy to use. There always has to be a compromise.

Fortunately for us, as EMM technology evolves, we have more options for how we actually make that compromise. Before MDM, the only choice was a BlackBerry. Then, once MDM came out, our range of options expanded to include iPhones or Android, but the compromise was that the device would still have to be locked down. Now MAM means that we don't have to lock down the device, but the compromise is that users have to use a third-party email client.

At this point, we need to think about what compromises are acceptable to ask of users. Can we ask them to put a password on their device? Perhaps a four-digit numeric pin is "reasonable," while a 12-character alphanumeric password with special characters is "unreasonable." How about app blacklisting? Can we tell them they can't have certain apps on their personal devices? That's probably a lot harder, and most likely no user will ever like that.

When thinking about the different options, I like to consider the fact that a MAM-based approach affects the user experience only while users are actually doing work on their devices. On evenings and weekends, everything is the same as it was before. Yes, a third-party email client might be cumbersome, but the user gets access to corporate resources without giving anything up the rest of the time, so it's a net gain. To put it another way, if something has to be locked down, I would want the default access technique to be something that doesn't degrade the experience for everything else a user does. Then, on the other hand, if a user decides he needs to be more productive and wants a native email experience, that user can make that choice and deal with the entire device being under tighter management.

The point here is that when there are multiple management options (and remember, we're mostly talking about email here), the best approach might be to make the default option the one with the least impact on the user. Then, if users decide they want another option, they can make the choice *on their own*, and then device-level management is introduced. The fact that a choice is offered (instead of IT forcing all users to go one way or another) is the most important part of this.

Different policies for BYOD?

As I mentioned in Chapter 10 and earlier in the book, the question of device ownership should come up only after many other technological issues have been resolved. (And when that happens, it's a good thing, because it signifies that you've covered a lot of ground with MDM, MAM, and dual persona!) That said, you do have to deal with BYOD eventually, and when you do, how can management policies differ for corporate devices versus user-owned ones?

First, consider the idea that the whole conversation about user experience and MAM versus MDM and different email techniques applies no matter who owns the device. So all that stuff about letting users choose how they access corporate resources is the same for corporate and personal devices. (And after all, if something is "secure enough" for BYOD, then it should be secure enough for corporate devices!)

Instead of basing policies on device ownership, a better way is to base them on how the device is used. There are all sort of different ways this could work: Certainly for shared devices, kiosks, and similar situations (which invariably involve corporate devices), tight device management is needed.

Then the next level of policy could be for "primary" devices, like the phones that people carry with them all the time. Here's where you could give users a choice in management techniques, regardless of who owns the device. Examples of this could be having IT manage a user's personal phone in order to provide as much access as possible to corporate resources, or it could mean using just MAM on a corporate phone (this would be that COPE idea—corporate owned, personally enabled—that we talked about earlier).

There could also be a set of policies for "secondary" devices that are used only to do work tasks occasionally. For example, I check my work email on my personal iPad a few times on the weekend, and every once in a while, I'll use it to log into BrianMadden. com to comment or fix a post. This occasional use doesn't need as much corporate access or management. One or two apps would suffice. (To be clear, this doesn't mean that IT should allow me to have unsecured email on the device, but rather if it just provided the managed browser and email client, I would be fine.)

Another way that policies might differ is for different types of devices, like whether a device is iOS or Android, what version of Android it is, or whether or not it supports third-party MDM APIs like Samsung SAFE.

The takeaway from all this is that the first consideration for making policies should be based on how devices are used or how they work, not whether the company bought them or the user did.

Making the expectations and risks clear

We know that mobility and combining work and personal tasks on a single device requires compromises, and that a good way to deal with those compromises is to offer users the choice of how they want to make that compromise (when possible). The goal for an IT department—working with HR—should be to figure out how to make these policies (and the reasons for them) very clear to users. If users understand that corporate data needs to be protected and IT offers reasonable methods and multiple choices (not just "we're going to lock down your phone"), this can be a good situation for everyone.

I can't stress enough how simple and plain your explanation needs to be, like, "If you don't have a passcode on your phone, and you leave your phone at a bar, someone could look at your email and leak the information to Wall Street, and we can get sued. We don't want that to be on you, so we make it that if you want to access your corporate email on your phone, you have to have a passcode."

Another plain-English explanation might be, "Did you know that many of the millions of apps out there can access your contacts and email and start doing bad things? Rather than you worrying about all the stuff you're downloading, we're just going to give you this alternate, secure email app for your work email. Then you can download whatever apps you want without having to worry about them stealing work stuff and getting us sued."

Or, "You know that we have to keep this information safe, but you can decide which of these ways you want to do it."

Policies like these should cover what you need and educate your users, but really, IT shouldn't have to deal with users all on its own. This is the time to get HR and the corporate lawyers to help out.

Dealing With the Continuing Effects of Consumerization

Even with clear policies and multiple options for users, IT still has to understand and accommodate the ongoing effects of the consumerization of IT.

In the beginning of the book, I wrote that a major shift occurred when users became able to access technology that was more advanced and powerful than the technology provided by IT. This inversion certainly caught us off guard and caused some of the chaos around consumerization in the past few years. But now that we know it happened and that it exists, we can figure out what to do about it.

So what exactly does it mean to "deal with consumerization?" It means being mindful of the gap that exists between technology provided by corporate IT and the technology that our users can go out and find on their own. No longer can we dig our heels in and say no to users. In today's work environment, we need to make a good-faith effort to not let that gap grow too big again, because when the gap is big, FUIT happens—users go rogue and figure out their own mobile solutions.

Let's use mobile file syncing as an example to illustrate what I'm talking about with this "gap" thing. If you ignore mobile file syncing and don't provide any way for your users to get their corporate files on their phones and tablets, you are 100% guaranteed that your users will find things like Dropbox on their own, since they have no other option. In that case, the gap between Dropbox and your 1990s-style SMB file share behind a VPN is just too big. The way you prevent that is to make sure that you also provide some kind of file syncing solution that works with mobile devices. The solution you provide doesn't have to "beat" Dropbox or be the best in every way—it just has to work kind of like Dropbox. Doing so helps close the gap between what you offer and what users can find on their own, thus minimizing the chances that they will go rogue and find their own solutions. That's what I mean by "minding the gap." (To be clear, you can never 100% prevent users from doing their own thing. That's the whole point of consumerization and FUIT. But minding the gap minimizes the chances that users will resort to FUIT.)

Today, a good-faith effort means more than just deploying some MDM and calling it a day. It means figuring out how to accommodate dual persona, BYOD, and mobile file syncing, and how to access other apps from mobile devices.

To be clear, none of this means that IT is totally giving up control—in fact, we do this to minimize the gap so that we can *maintain* control. Of course we still need to protect corporate data. But now, instead of completely trying to lock down every single device that comes into our environment, we instead concentrate more on the data (and the apps) that we actually care about. We keep the important stuff protected while making it accessible enough so that users don't have to forcibly break it out to get their jobs done.

Keep in mind that one of the realities of consumerization is that you don't always have control over user-created content. This is not a new problem, and it certainly existed long before consumerization. You can encourage users to do all of their work with official apps, but at the end of the day, if users want to take meeting notes in Evernote or store documents they wrote in Dropbox, there's nothing you can really do about that. Some companies try to work out these crazy systems where they attempt to intercept and encrypt everything users create before it can get to Dropbox, but that's kind of missing the point and ultimately futile. The overall goal for IT should be to provide officially sanctioned corporate solutions that are as good as other solutions and as easy to use as possible (here's that "mind the gap" concept again) so that hopefully users will choose them for the work-related content they create on their own. However, you still need to accept and be able to deal with this not always being the case.

Finally, it should be clear by now that dealing with consumerization means that you shouldn't care as much about what users are doing on the personal stuff on their devices. Instead, the perimeter of what you care about and really control shrinks down to just the important data and apps.

12. The Future of Enterprise Mobility Management

Most of what we've been talking about throughout this entire book is based on technologies that have been around only for a few years, so it's natural to wonder where it's all going. I'm not going to try to make any grand predictions, but I can look at some of the things that have been covered in this book and outline different ways they could evolve.

How the Current EMM Framework Could Mature

Let's first look at several ways that EMM could continue along its current path and evolve in the short term.

MAM standards

There's a lot to like about MAM, but as we discussed, there are still pain points around acquiring MAM-compatible apps. This is why the idea of open standards for MAM is so appealing. With MAM standards, any app that was intended to be used as a corporate app could be built with a standardized SDK or app wrapping tool so that it could be managed by any EMM platform. (And think about it, iOS and Android can be managed by different vendors' products, so why not apps?) This would have benefits for all parties involved:

- ISVs wouldn't have to worry about aligning with one MAM vendor or another or worry about making multiple versions of their apps. Instead, if they want to target an app for enterprise users, they could use one set of MAM features and still have it work with any EMM solution.
- End users would have more choice over which apps they use to get their jobs done. Imagine if companies or end users could choose between dozens of different email apps or document editors, all 100% compatible with whatever MAM product they're using and all right there in the public app store (where they go to get all of their other apps, anyway).
- IT wouldn't have to worry about being locked in to a particular EMM vendor.
- MAM vendors could all boast a wide range of compatible apps and compete on other aspects of their solutions. It's a "rising tide raises all ships" situation.

Unfortunately, getting dozens of vendors to agree and implement common standards doesn't happen overnight, and the track record for standards consortiums is mixed. But VHS won out over Betamax, Blu-ray Disc beat out HD DVD, and all our mobile devices use the same Wi-Fi standards, so there's hope that either informal (through natural market forces, acquisitions, or licensing) or formal standards for MAM could emerge.

Will it ever happen? It's too early to tell. So far, MobileIron is the only vendor really talking about open MAM standards with its Open App Alliance.

iOS 7 and the next version of Android

We'll know more about the impact of iOS 7 in the fall when it's released publicly, but with the loosening of restrictions around multitasking, there's potential for third-party email clients to become much more acceptable to users.

Aside from iOS multitasking, a lot of people are wondering if changes in iOS 7 and the next version of Android could cause a major shift in the EMM world. While there's a lot that we don't know yet, and certainly there will be new interesting features, there's nothing that indicates these OSes will become fully enabled for dual persona à la Samsung KNOX or BlackBerry Balance. Yes, there might be some shift in the balance between MDM and MAM, but all of the concepts covered in this book will still matter. There will still be a need to manage apps and devices, and to provide mobile access to corporate resources.

The role of specialty dual persona devices

What about the role of specialty dual persona devices, like Samsung KNOX or VMware Horizon Mobile? While these are great in some situations, for the near future, we have to consider these devices the exception, not the rule. This means that we have to put effort into MAM solutions that can accommodate dual persona on any type of device.

EMM feature wish list

Those who have been working with EMM for a while (or who are reading this book) can probably come up with a long list of features that would make their lives easier. Every time new versions of iOS and Android come out, there are always many articles with feature wish lists. I don't want to go too crazy, but here are a few things I'd like to see in the future:

- More granular policies for Exchange ActiveSync. Remember that device access rules can get pretty specific, but Exchange allows only one device management policy per mailbox, so once a user is allowed to connect, all of that user's devices get the same policies. It would be nice to have per-device policies for a single user/mailbox.
- I'd like more features for the Device Administration API in the core version of Android, such as settings for mail accounts, VPNs, and Wi-Fi.
- I'd also love to see granular app permissions in Android, with the ability to control individual aspects of what an app can do, such as access to contacts, photos, and location data. Features like this are already available in modified versions of Android (such as CyanogenMod), so hopefully it can make it into regular Android. This has happened with other features before, so there's hope.

Moving Beyond Our Current Framework to Mobile Information Management

Are there any alternatives to the current EMM framework outlined in this book? Or what will happen to EMM in the more distant future?

One concept that many people talk about is mobile information management (MIM). This is the idea that management policies can be directly embedded into data itself, making it secure no matter where it goes and which applications use it. This seems pretty logical. After all, we moved from device-level management down to app-level management, so the next step would be shrinking the perimeter even more so we're just managing the data, right?

The problem is that there has to be a compromise somewhere. Keeping data both completely secured and allowing it to flow anywhere and be manipulated by any app is an impossible paradox.

Ultimately, you have to be able to know or trust the app that's being used to manipulate the data so that you can be sure it's respecting the management policies.

Let's take Exchange ActiveSync as an example of this. When the protocol delivers email messages to a client, it can also specify certain management policies like passwords or encryption, and the protocol can also be used to wipe the client. But the key to making this work is that the client has to be designed specifically to work with the protocol, and it has to be licensed to do so. This is all well and good, but unfortunately, we're already seeing this get broken. In some of the underground app stores, we're seeing mail clients that lie to the Exchange Server. They'll report that they have enabled a device password or that they have remotely wiped a device, when in reality they have not. And the EAS protocol is clearly insufficient for managing some clients (like iOS and Android devices, which is why we to manage them separately with MDM!)

So this means that for any form of MIM, we need clients that are designed to work with the data, and we need to trust that they will execute our policies faithfully. This means we might have to only allow certain clients to access the data, and maybe manage those clients—and by that point we're right back at MAM.

However, widespread MAM standards could act like MIM. A user could take any app built to work with MAM and use it to access corporate resources. That app might not have been intended for that specific user or company, but if the company's EMM platform can recognize that the app will respect its policies, then it can allow the app to access corporate resources.

On another front, many apps are becoming much more closely tied to the data that they create, consume, and manipulate. For example, what type of files does Evernote use? I have no idea. I just know that the application Evernote has all my notes in it. All that matters is that I have the app, an Internet connection, and my login credentials. As more apps behave this way, the distinction between managing apps and managing data is less important. The apps and data become inseparable.

Conclusion

By now we've considered a wide range of ways to approach mobile devices. You should be better equipped to consider products from different EMM vendors, support mobile devices, and deal with BYOD.

What has made an impression on me while covering EMM and writing this book is how genuinely excited people are about mobility. Dozens of IT pros, users, executives, EMM vendors, and ISVs have all expressed optimism about the great things that it can do for them.

So where do you start? While everybody's requirements are different, I like to keep a few basic points in mind:

- Approach mobility as an issue of providing access to apps and data, not locking down endpoints.
- Remember that BYOD is not a big deal. The bulk of what you do will apply to any device, no matter who owns it.
- Mobile devices are completely different from desktops, but can be used to do just as much work.
- While you can't build an entire corporate app ecosystem in a day, mail apps, file syncing, and secure browsers are easy wins. Especially file syncing—do that one now.
- Your approach to email (and tolerance for how open it is) will have a large impact on your environment.
- Consumerization is a two-way street. You need to make sure your users understand the need to keep resources safe, but you also need to make corporate resources accessible. You can't "beat" consumerization, but you can avoid FUIT by making a good-faith effort to allow users to work in modern ways.

* * *

The nature of work is changing. It's up to us to make sure that our users can take advantage of all the benefits of modern mobility. Good luck!

Jack Madden
@jackmadden
July 2013